Divorced, Now What?

Dating in Your 30s, 40s, 50s & Beyond

I0516895

Lynn Morgan

Copyright © 2025 by Lynn Morgan

All Rights Reserved

No portion of this book may be reproduced in any form without written permission from the publisher or author, except as permitted by copyright law.

First Edition 2025

Dedicate this book to my young, adult children:

Always believe in yourself and love will come.

ACKNOWLEDGEMENTS

This book is dedicated to my daughter and son, Morgan and Carmen. They are outstanding young adults, and it's been an honor to be their mother. I couldn't be prouder!! They are healthy, intelligent, contributing members of society. Never lose your integrity.

We have made it through the years since their father and I split, and they were so very young. I did the best I could all these years. It takes a village. God bless you both.

ABOUT THE AUTHOR

Lynn grew up in the suburbs of Baltimore. Since she comes from an Irish Catholic family, she never thought she would be divorced. Her motto is everything happens for a reason. Turn lemons into lemonade, as they say. Now, she resides in Abingdon, MD, and enjoys working out, dining out, and traveling. She wishes everyone to learn, grow, and live a joyful life.

PREFACE

As the new year approaches, it is always a time for reflection, regrouping, and figuring out where I am headed.

My career started out as a programmer/analyst and I ended up divorced with two wonderful children, a daughter and a son, who are very intelligent, funny, and kind. I am blessed and know that. Yet, being divorced, I thought life would be different. Instead, here I am.

At the beginning of every new year, you look at where you have been, where you want to go, and hopefully, come up with a plan on how to get there. Though, that's not always easy. As I reflected, I thought, *"Divorced...now what?"* and that is what led me to write this book. *Who am I? Where am I? What am I doing? Where am I headed? What do I want out of life, especially personally and how do we get there?*

CHAPTER 1

GROWING UP

Growing up, I was a small kid who learned to entertain herself. I was the only child from a broken home like many children of my generation. My parents met, married, and had me when they were young. Unfortunately, it didn't work out and my parents separated when I was eighteen months old. I lived with my mother, who had full physical custody and saw my father on scheduled weekly visits for five hours each Sunday. It truly didn't leave a lot of bonding time.

I went to a private Catholic elementary school and later high school as well. I received all the sacraments growing up and did the whole "Catholic thing." I believe to this day that the Catholic guilt is ingrained in me. I have gotten tremendously better, but it has been a struggle. Although I attended two private Catholic schools, my family was not wealthy by any means. I grew up in an apartment for my first 26 years of life. I didn't know what it was like to play in a yard or have more than one floor where you lived. Instead, it was a two-bedroom, one-bathroom apartment. There were hardly any children growing up in the apartments at that time. Maybe more nowadays due to the higher divorce rate, economy, etc., they are. Being the only child and my mother working fulltime, I entertained myself with books, puzzles, whatever I could, etc. Often, there were not playmates outside to spend time with. I took ballet and tap lessons for many years, which did not help with my coordination, I might add. I couldn't be involved in clubs because many made you stay after school. No one could pick me up after the regular time, so how could I? I didn't really participate in sports until high school, even though many arrangements had to be made.

Although the divorce rate was slowly rising as I was growing, I was one of the very few who had divorced parents during elementary school. Of course, children won't have divorced parents. That was almost hypocritical back then. My mother worked full time and I went to different sitters. Back then, there weren't, but a few licensed daycare centers and forget preschools or before or after care as they are referred to today. I had "winter sitters," those women who watched me during the school year, and "summer sitters," those who watched me during the summer because the winter ones made plans with their families. I had more "sitters" than anyone. I am neither complaining nor saying it was bad. Just saying you felt shuffled. Hard to explain, Miss Nancy in the summer, Miss Kitty in the winter.

CHAPTER 2

FAST FORWARD

Here I am, 53, how many years alone now? I seem to be dating guys, but it's always around New Year's Eve when they're not around or we break up. LOL. Ultimately, I am alone. I hate this day as a runner-up to Valentine's Day.

That being said, I started revamping my life. On December 19th, 2022, I decided to reactivate my Match.com membership. In January 2022, I began a membership for six months. No doubt, I had some good dates and some interesting experiences. I think I met about five guys. Two of them I dated more than a few dates. I'll elaborate more later. When I reactivated it, you don't have to pay anything. Apparently, I got "like" some messages. Of course, with the percentage off because I can be frugal, I decided to do it on

New Year's Eve 2022. May this adventure begin...

Here we go. I'm going to go on each and every one of my dates and take notes. I'm going outside of Harford County, MD, to meet men. In this county, I can't seem to find what I want. I know I am all that and you may think that's being conceited. Forget the degrees or professional training. Forget I consider myself slender, though I am not built like Barbie in the upper chest cavity. I'm attractive, have a sense of humor, intelligent, kind, and generous. I'm tired of being taken for granted by men. Let me just say that. I will say it again... I am tired of being taken for granted by men. How do you feel, ladies?

I will say this... never lose lope! Always believe... learn and grow along the way. Live your life and laugh.

CHAPTER 3

JAIME, THE ONE THAT WASN'T

ALL THAT

I got out of a relationship right before COVID and the guy kept coming around promised me the Moon. Believe me, I'm never dating a "separated" guy again... never NEVER. That guy and I were seven years apart, and knew each other for 14 as friends socially. He was married, I could tell he wasn't happy, he would vent, I would listen. We all met in a group like 10 of us out.

What do I say to ANY married person having trouble? Go to counseling. Work it out, grass isn't greener. Though, I must admit, more often than not things can't be worked, unfortunately.

This man, Jaime, I knew for 14 years out and about in the local town social scene. Yes, I knew he was married. The group of girlfriends I hang with, we all knew he was. There were married men that we knew, said hello to, and some even gave us a hug. All platonic. He and I spoke while spotting each other out. It was the usual hi, how are you, how's the wife, my kids, work. That was it! Then, I hear through the grapevine, he moves out. I see him out and he asks, will you go out with me? I said, well, you still live there, and he says: Oh no, I moved out. I wanted him to confirm what I had heard. We exchanged numbers and started conversing only after he moved out. He was in a state of transition, as anyone is during the separation process. He had no children with this spouse, no investments, and a townhouse to sell. Unfortunately, that took a year to sell. In the meantime, we dated, had dinners, lunches, drinks, and heard live music. May I say he was a wonderful dancer! Not many men are, just saying.

That's hard to find a male who likes to dance. We have many common interests. They included boating, biking as in going on his Harley-Davidson, dinners, dancing, chilling, watching movies. He had been a friend many years and our friendship grew closer. We talked about many, many things including the future. He is the one who always brought up the future and said many times, not just once, I'm going get divorced, move in, and give you a ring to propose. (Boy, I was a fool.)

OK OK I didn't have to get married. All of my GFs know that marriage wasn't my goal. It wasn't a must!! I simply want a commitment. It could be living together; that would have been sufficient. Some type of ring would have been even better! Was I being materialistic? No. My point is for him to put his money where his mouth was. Commit if you really want the relationship, and he said this many times!! I knew I didn't imagine it. In the end, I found out others heard him say it as well. We continued to date and about every three months, I would bring up the subject of divorce. He would get mad, an argument ensued, we broke up at least three times. Finally, after two years and nine months, I had had it! I broke up with him a few days before Valentine's Day in 2020. I told him that was it, I am done, I don't need this. He told me so many things. That was it.

Another month later COVID sets in, March 2020. He was kind, he stayed in touch, my daughter came home from college, my son's high school stopped, and the world came to a stop. As we know, the world went virtual. He would spring for food and with two teenagers, I always welcome food, I am human!! LOL We are all foodies in this household.

We would talk from a distance, literally like from the front door to the kitchen. He invited me over where he was living, we would talk outside and have a bite to eat, and hang out. I still enjoyed his company, just not the promises.

Now, I know what you're thinking as you read this... why did this woman who is intelligent, has a personality, had raised children essentially solo decide to linger in this relationship? Not sure. I thought that many, many times myself. Obviously, he was a friend, we enjoyed each other's company, and had fun! That's that. I did love him. He was a companion and there was chemistry. Perhaps, there was even passion? He was muscular, in very good shape for his age, good looking. He was protective. I do believe he loved me, even in the end.

I am human and we had a ton in common!! There was a connection and chemistry. Of course, we loved one another. Yet is that enough? Think about that...all of you reading this book. More on that later. Can love truly be enough?

Time went on and he didn't follow through. Same old song and dance! DONE!!! I told him that is it... again! Many months later, summer, fall, I really couldn't date. Wasn't into it. Though I met a few people outside just to socialize.

You could tell Jaime loved me, it was very apparent, and I loved him. People told me all the time. No lie. But can I tell you, ladies? Make a man keep his word!! ALWAYS!!! We are worth it. Hold him to it. Did I say give him an ultimatum? NO. Set your boundaries, always.

That's exactly what I did. It took me too long, I'm the one who suffered, put myself through heck. People had to tell me, which I already knew. I had already done it. They just reassured me after the fact. I spent way too much time on him and with him.

Then, Autumn, 2020, is here. Next thing I know... He kept staying in touch with me and tells me he's sick. I tell him it sounds like you have COVID from the symptoms he describes.

This was on a Monday, and on Thursday, he finally got tested. Yes, he did have it. I dropped him off groceries as a friend, he was having trouble breathing. The next day I find out he's in a local hospital near where he was renting. Let's just cut to the end. That local hospital isn't known to be the best. He is instant messaging me, "not doing good. Not sure I am going to make it through the night." Now, let's remember, even though we are broken up, I still care for him as a friend. By this time, we've known each other 17 years at least. I certainly did not want him to die. He kept saying how he couldn't breathe. His lungs were filled with fluid. The whole time, he kept eating though, which was good and he had a fever they couldn't get rid of. COVID was only six months old, here in the U.S., and we still didn't know much about it.

In the meantime, he must have given the wife his username and password to post his status on Facebook and ask for prayers. He denied to me that he gave it to her. Now, I am no Facebook, or technology expert, but I could tell though via the posts that she had his account information. Regardless, I still prayed for him. That's what I do!! I pray about everything. I even went to downtown

Baltimore, which is no easy feat considering the crime, and attended mass at St. Jude Shrine, which is nationally known. I lit candles and I do absolutely believe in the power of prayer. Ultimately, I do believe all the prayers saved him. The wife is posting updates every other day. It got to be a little bit much. In that, she was being very descriptive. I told him I can't believe you're allowing her to post some very private details of your medical status. This is a very proud and vain man. It just did not make sense. Why do that to someone? No one had to know this poor man had a catheter, he's close to death, and you're posting this? Are you freaking kidding me? Is there no discretion? That should tell you something right there!

He felt he got great care at that local hospital near his place; he was in there a week. He went back to where he was renting, though he continued to have breathing problems. People were checking on him, he continued to monitor his pulse, check his temperature, etc. Remember, we still don't know much about COVID seven months in.

He and I would text since he was back at his place, bored, restless, and he still wasn't 100%. Since he's having trouble breathing, he plans to go to the University of Maryland. He can't catch his breath. He gets down there and they discover he has multiple blood clots that the first hospital didn't catch.

You all are reading this thinking so what? Why is she telling people about this? I am telling you for a few reasons. One being though we were broken up he continued to text me and call me twice a day Two, though the wife was ruling Facebook, telling the world intimate details, I was on his mind. Three, KNOW your body, people. He did!

Since they weren't divorced yet, he was still under her health insurance, and she was his advocate. However, did she really fulfill that role? I say that because he was keeping me informed every day while he was at that first hospital. He needed oxygen and they told him he would need oxygen. Yet, what happened? He was discharged without it. WTH? He had to be his own advocate. He thought she would be it, but I got news for you. I was texting him questions that no one thought of nor had answers to. Again, why didn't she make sure or ask where's the oxygen? What are his stats?

I was not that surprised when he had to go to another hospital, be there another five days, what was discovered, and guess what? He was sent home THIS TIME WITH OXYGEN. He also couldn't be alone when he was discharged. He would have to go to rehab, or to family or friends. Since the person he was renting from worked two jobs and was hardly there, that wasn't optimal, and he ended up going to a relative's house. My only point to this whole story folks is: BE YOUR OWN ADVOCATE. He thought his supposed wife was his advocate. Yet, was she? I was asking him questions that no one was asking. I later found out, he posed those same questions to her. OOOOOPPPPSSS!!

Lesson: we all know our own bodies, we listen, and are aware. Insist upon medical attention for your own body. Be your own advocate and line up someone to speak on your behalf in case you cannot.

Guess what happened then! What are you thinking folks? Yes, she contacted me not once, but three times via instant messenger on Facebook. After the third time, I blocked her and said that's it. He's on his own. By this time, it's January through March of 2021. We are done. Been done for at least the fifth time by now. Lol! I only have myself to blame. Really, I am intelligent, very independent, and financially stable that I do not need a man.

Fast forward a few months. I heard through the grapevine he was getting better. I blocked him on instant messenger via Facebook and Facebook itself along with texting. It was Mother's Day weekend of 2021, and he just appears at my front door. I was actually talking to friends of mine on the phone, and they said be careful blah blah blah blah blah. He has stored a lot of his stuff here. He had a storage unit, but if you recall, he was supposed to move in. Some was in the garage; some was in the back basement in storage; other items were in closets. A lot of it was downstairs in the basement. After sitting at the kitchen table and talking two hours, he says will you help me move my stuff out? I looked at him and I said, I don't want to help you, but I will because you're sick. He was still recovering. He got winded very easily especially going up and down steps. I helped him make at least three trips. He loaded in his truck, and I went for a walk. He says, "Well, I'll be here when you get back." I told him there's no need. I said, "Please be gone as soon as you pack up."

He left wrought iron patio furniture on my deck, two area rugs in my living room and dining room that match perfectly I might add! Clothes, shoes, just different things, books, you name it. We're done and had been done!!

Ironically, I didn't get upset. The crying was over. From a man who promised me all these things that never came to fruition, I was over him. From saying he was going to move in, to commit to me, go on trips. It was all complete and utter bullshit! I am telling you, ladies, he wasn't done with the wife as much as he was saying he was! Emotionally especially. Oh, well.

On another note, I was never introduced to his family!!! HUGE RED FLAG!!!! TAKE NOTE. After that amount of time, you should meet his family. He had two sisters and a brother. The one sister he's particularly close to accused me of things weren't that weren't true, and he told me. I really feel it was a mistake he told me. He was not being honest with her and standing up for me. ANOTHER HUGE RED FLAG!!! Girlfriends, can I say, the man has to introduce you to the family. Now, there is being too long and there's being too quick. I'll fill you in on the differences between the two with a quick story later.

Was it for the best? No doubt. But, let me tell you ladies, you don't know that going through the situation. You can read these words from what I write, and think, wow, this woman's dumb!! I had never had a connection like that. I didn't have it with my ex-husband, or anyone that I had dated. There you have it.

LET'S FAST FORWARD AGAIN. That was May 2021. Summer goes by, then Fall, and then, it's January 2022. He contacts me out of the blue! Hey look that rhymes. LOL!

See, I amuse myself! I know you are thinking... WTH? Me too! I was done. What happened?

He contacts me and calls me and it's like 6:45 in the morning. I just got out of the shower. I don't pick up, let it go to voicemail. Not five minutes later, I get a text saying, 'Good morning, can you please call me? I really need to speak with you.' I have to get out the door for work, I don't have time for this nonsense. About 7:45 a.m., I call him back, I say, "You only have the car ride from here to work because I have to go in and I have a conference call." He proceeds to tell me how much he cares about me, he misses me, he is sorry for all the hurt that he put me through. I thank him, tell him I have to go. I say take care, feel better, and I will continue to pray. I go about my day, my week, a couple of weeks.

Here it is February 2022. Meanwhile, Jamie sees my girlfriends out and about in our local town. I was kind of avoiding spots and staying in as I do. I tend to be Cancer, the crab of my zodiac sign, and stay in during the winter. He speaks with a few of my friends. He tries to get information from them, find out what I'm doing, if I'm with anyone.

I go to a local non-denominational church for Monday evening service. I come out on a Monday night and there are flowers on my car. They are regular store-bought flowers from the grocery store. They were dyed daisies in pink, red, and white. They were nice, not my style, no card accompanied them. I looked at the girlfriend who was with me at church and she looked at me and said, "Oh no I think it's my fault." Rosemary says he's been asking about you, and I told him, "You're fine, and he askswhen do I see you? I told him we go to Monday church together."

I just replied to her, "OK just don't tell him anymore." I never communicated to him that I received these. I didn't want it to start all over. Let's keep things as they were. Things have been calm for quite some time. I appreciated the normalcy and peace.

Two days later, after I arrived home after working a nine-and-a-half-hour day, I pull in the driveway and not completely into my garage. It was a Wednesday evening and I always roll out the trash and recycles before going in for the night. There was a different car parked in front of the house beside me. However, that house was for sale, and I thought someone was touring that home. When I was retrieving items off of my passenger seat, I turned and he's right at my car door. Can you say CREEPY? He proceeded to ask me what was wrong. How come I didn't contact him? Did I get the flowers? I replied you left those flowers, there was no card to know! He says he loves me and wants to try again! I looked at him and I said, "Do you not remember we are done?" I asked if he was divorced yet? Now, that's the clincher. Of course not! He swore he would be!!! Let me remind you... It was over four and a half years that we had started dating by this point and he's still not divorced. I reminded him that he's the one who came it moved his stuff out 10 months prior and said that was it!!! Now, he's ready to try again. Are you serious?? He ended up being in my driveway for 45 minutes, he wanted to come in and I would not let him. I came in to let the dog out. "It's done," I say, "you still have not made no progress!!" Finally, he leaves, I come in, lock all the doors, and go upstairs to change out of work clothes. Whew! What an evening!

Here it is the following Monday again. It happens to be two days before Valentine's Day and I'm at church again with my girlfriend, Rosemary. We were talking after church, and I went out to my car before she did. I happen to park in a totally different spot and area than what I normally do. I get to my car and what's on the front windshield? Come on... guess! Work with me, ladies. A dozen long stem red roses in a clear glass vase with two cards. They sit on my front windshield. I look at it and I start to fill up. Am I sad? No! I'm angry. At this point, he has crossed a boundary. Not once, but twice! You never ever go to someone's place where they worship. That's an invasion of space, boundaries, etc. I go back into the building, Rosemary can see I'm frustrated. I told her you're going walk out to my car with me so you can serve as a witness not once, but twice. I wanted her as a witness should I have to get some sort of protective order. I went home, opened the cards. It was funny; one was quite serious that he was professing his love to me. Let's recall... he's still not divorced!! That was the kicker.

I see him out and about the following week at a local establishment and he pulls me aside to talk to me. I tell him, "You're still not divorced you promised me all this."

Once again, LET'S FAST FORWARD. In July of 2022, I see him add another local hangout and he keeps going up to this girl with long dark hair. I don't think she's that attractive or his type. Whatever, I couldn't care less. Guess what? She has the same first name as me!! Lol! Good luck with that one!! Coincidence or not?

CHAPTER 4

WILLIAM

About 10 years ago, I had a date with a gentleman named William. We met through a dating site back then. He was from the area, we sent a few emails, and decided to meet. We had one date, it was short. I didn't think he was for me. I really think it was bad timing on both of our parts. I was too busy raising kids.

Fast forward about 10 years, we have stayed in touch, text here and there, seeing each other out, waved across the room. He kept reaching out to me for about eight months. He knew I dated Jamie, and wanted to make sure I was really over him!! I told him at least a half dozen times I was. He kept checking on me during the winter months, texting me here and there, around the holidays, etc. Time moves on. He asked me out once in March and another date in April. Then, I don't hear from him again and he ghosts me.

He texted me Happy Mother's Day. When Father's Day came around, I texted him Happy Father's Day. He finally asked me out again, and we start dating. We have mutual interests; he's a little quiet at first, but he started opening up. He happened to be nine years older than me. That doesn't bother me. Let me just say this though, ladies, it doesn't mean he's mature at all! Live and learn lesson like #23! Laughing yet?

Lesson: A man must be mature in many ways. It must not be all about him either.

We would go out to dinners, on his boat, take a ride on his Harley-Davidson, hang out, and watch movies. He didn't work out the way I like to work out. Yet, his career and business required him to be in shape to a point.

He was quiet, way more introverted than I. He was very different. He had his own business and was a machinist, more on the blue-collar line. He was not dumb by any means. He had a good heart, which is hard to find in this day and age. He looked after an elderly aunt, took her to the doctors, errands, everything. He had the patience of a saint in those situations. When friends found out we were dating, someone even said he has a "kind soul." It started off nice, content, and I had hope! That didn't last.

We had arguments and major disagreements. He didn't like then I went to happy hours after work for networking events. He thought I was always picking up men, and eventually, it became a source of contention. I told him he had to trust me. Multiple times, he would accuse me of ignoring him, not picking up the phone, or not replying to his text right away. You're always hanging at the bars. This all got old very quickly. I don't need someone controlling me. I had that with my ex-husband!! Needless to say, the relationship wasn't off to a good start. We had fun, but it seemed like things were always ending in an argument or with tense words. He was constantly accusing me of going out and being at the bars and I was going to happy hours to network. I didn't need to be accused of stuff. We still went out; he was extremely jealous and insecure. I couldn't stand it!!! Please, can I tell you—the insecurity must go! That is a red flag right there. I didn't walk, I ran!! It wasn't getting better. It got worse after his heart surgery, absolutely worse! I felt like I was married to my ex-husband all over again. I started losing myself, doubting myself. I was accused of picking up people.

Well, we were sitting there watching a movie and he was kind of grabbing his chest, having trouble breathing. I didn't say anything then. I let it go, and I said you really should get checked out. That was like two months into dating. I also noticed we didn't go out on the boat as much because every time it was really humid, he was having trouble breathing. We would just go to dinner, have a few drinks, and hang out. During Labor Day weekend, it worsened, and I told him he had to get it checked out or else I would break up. I couldn't stand it anymore. I certainly didn't want to be with an old man, nor did he act like an old man until this. You could tell something was seriously wrong. We stayed together each night during Labor Day weekend because I was really scared for him. Something was wrong!!! The dead ringer was when he complained of indigestion and acid reflux after dinner one night. He ended up eating a whole roll of Rolaids. Say it with me, HUGE RED FLAG! Keep in mind, we dated barely three months.

Tuesday after Labor Day weekend, he swears to me that morning he's driving himself to a hospital further away than our local one that specializes in the heart. I said fine, I will pray, good luck. He is texting me all through the day. He is telling me they are testing for this or that, EKG, stress test blah blah blah. Not 45 minutes after his last text, I've received a call from a number I don't recognize on my cell phone. It's his sister telling me that they are admitting him, and it looks like he needs a double bypass. After my regular day at work, I let the dog out, feed him, and go on to the hospital that night and the next night. The following morning, he was in surgery at 7:00 a.m., it was very evident he was scared to death. I support him through all this. I probably would do it all over again. We were friends for years. After having a quadruple bypass, not a double pass as originally told, he was in the hospital a week, got discharged, and went to a family member's home to recover. I went there both days of every weekend for about a month. I bought him special pillows for him to rest his arm, clothes, made him food. I was there. During his recovery, the accusations subsided. That's because I was always there on the weekends. During the week, he knew I was working, and I was home in the evening. Things were peaceful. I thought we were growing closer, and he knew I was there for him. I mean I was!!

Then, after a month, he returns to his home to recover. Again, I make him meals, buy him comfy clothes, etc. I even start to clean his house and I mean clean it. He had cleaning people come every week until his surgery. He wasn't home for a bit or working and making money, so he had them stop. I figured I'd do that for him. I don't clean for anybody!! LOL. He wasn't even appreciative of that.

One Thursday evening, he invited me to come over and watch a movie. He knew I was going to run two errands after work that being Walmart and the grocery store, come home, unload, change, and go to his house. I was running about 15 minutes late, I text him that, he called. I get to his house, and he texted me you should not come over tonight. I replied too late I just pulled in your driveway. He was in his truck on the other end. I mean, he barely talked to me. I thought OK, he's just getting back into working a little bit, he's still in pain. We were talking and he growled at me. Keep in mind prior to his surgery, I was accused of this, that, and the other. Many guy friends said that's a sign of immaturity and insecurity, even leading to jealousy. I did end up hanging out, watching a movie. He fell asleep within the first 15 minutes. I fell asleep on the sofa, and I should have gotten up and left. I didn't get three hours of sleep that night. I was afraid to leave him alone, just in case, because I knew he was so scared and in pain as a complication after surgery. He didn't know I left, doesn't call me for hours later, and acts like everything's fine.

Let me back up. When I was at his house and he growled at me, it was because he stated he called, and I didn't pick up the phone. I replied I did, and we talked. He stated no, he called before that. I showed him my phone and that I had no missed calls from him!! He wouldn't look at the phone, he still kept accusing me. It was all I could do just to have peace. Then, he fell asleep. So what company was that? Aggravation and then none!! I should never have gone over. I was also accused of trying to meet up with someone when he knew I was at Walmart and the grocery store, and I brought him items from both places. Go figure!!

I guess that last example was the straw that broke the camel's back, as they say. I told him this wasn't working. I didn't realize how stressed I was... until I wasn't!! Didn't realize why my hair was falling out, so well guess what? A few months later, it completely stopped falling out.

It got back to me after we stopped dating that he was talking about me at bars. One evening, I was trying to get ahold of him, and he didn't answer my call, then I would text him. A female mutual friend we know asked him who's that? He replied and told her it was me. Then, he told her, I don't feel like answering. How rude and disrespectful is that!! Embarrassing as well!! Let's not forget, he accused me of going to bars and he was at a bar when I'm trying to get ahold of him. I am all concerned, offering to make him dinner. Another time, he told people oh she wants me to go slow until December. That's just tough. I am going to find a woman that wants me now. Again, that is totally disrespectful, rude, and discourteous. I deserve way more respect!! As we all do, ladies! I ran from this one. LOSER with a capital L.

Here this guy is nine years older, and he is immature as heck, and he proved it! In the county I am in, all they do is gossip. Very done with it and especially the gossip.

Can we see the similarities in these last two men I have dated? Grant, they are older, but both are immature, they don't mean what they say, say things that demonstrate their insecurity. The kicker is I didn't go after these men! They came after me. Am I giving out asshole radar wanted or what? That's something for me to ponder in the new year. The first guy, Jamie, Rosemary swears he was looking at me for years. He would even tell me what outfits I wore when he saw me out and about in the group. Was he stalking me? No, I don't think so. Apparently, I must have left a deep impression in his mind. Nonetheless, what are these men thinking? Do they not realize what they do or really say? Are they just words to convince women? I truly don't understand. I stood by William throughout his surgery and everything else.

Let me finish the story about William. That was it, I told him we were over, he has no clue why I was so upset. All we did was text back and forth. It was almost like a text war. I would ignore him, and he would keep texting. Did he ever call? It took him three weeks to actually pick up the phone and call me. Suddenly, he wanted to work at the relationship. He wanted to get together, he wanted to go to dinner, anything I wanted. I reminded him that I asked him repeatedly, many, many times to trust me and I told him where I was going and what I was doing. It was never enough. If it wasn't enough now, it never will be! After all, it took him three weeks to hit that green button on the phone and talk. It was too late. I'm not a needy, high-maintenance woman. I'm independent, keep myself entertained, and busy. But, if you didn't get a clue even in that amount of time, I don't even feel sorry for you!!!

FAST FORWARD AGAIN!! A few weeks later, what happens? I run an errand after a 10-hour workday, come home, and change. I see there's a box on the front steps from ProFlowers. I bring it in, open it up, and there are two dozen long stem red roses with a vase. The card attached says how much he misses me and loves me.

Lesson: Ladies, let me tell you... if a guy misses you and truly loves you, he won't be accusing you all the time. He will trust you! He will want to see you again, most definitely.

You will feel relaxed, will want to laugh, and have fun! Instead, I couldn't wait to get to my own home!

After I put the roses in each of their vases, I heated up dinner, and just as I set it on the table, the dog goes ballistic. Someone's knocking on my side lights next to my front door. Any guesses who? That's right, you guessed it, it's William!

Another guy who doesn't respect boundaries and who just shows up! I open the door because I know he won't leave until I do so, but I do not let him. He's standing by the storm door. He's asking me won't I let him in? I replied no! He says won't you give me a hug and the kiss? And I said no. You could tell he had been crying; his eyes were all bloodshot. He apologized like ten times. I said you just don't get it do you? It's ridiculous! In the meantime, in those few brief moments before he showed up after I finished organizing the flowers, I took a picture of the roses and sent it to my girlfriend, Rosemary. She commented deja vu! Lol, but so not!

While he was here, I had my cell phone in my hand. I accidentally hit it so that I called her number, totally unintentional. She heard the conversation back and forth. It was not going well, I could not get rid of him! She asked if I was OK, and I said yes. She said I'm coming over and I went OK. He ended up being here a total of 4o minutes, I did get rid of him in the end. She did show up with her dog within three minutes after he left. Nonetheless it was creepy, unwarranted, and complete violation of boundaries. I blocked him on Facebook, messenger, and the cell phone number. I guess that wasn't enough.

I proceeded to get three more cards from him, a handwritten note thanking me for everything. He also kept calling me from different cell phone numbers and texting me. He was asking me to his family's Thanksgiving dinner which was held a week before Thanksgiving. By this time, we had been broken up a month or more, and he didn't tell his family we were over. He still wanted me to go. I looked at him and I said, "Didn't you tell your family we are not together?" His family has to know how he is with women. I got news for you... I was the best women he ever dated and will be!! I don't need the accusations and everything else.

Lesson: If the person you are dating, male or female, is that insecure, immature, and generally, does not trust you, it will NEVER work, EVER.

Trust is the root of the relationship. Then, when the person is talking about you in a disrespectful and unfavorable way, keep walking away and don't look back.

CHAPTER 5

NEW YEAR'S EVE 2022

I decided it was time for a change. Time to shake things up a bit. On December 20th, 2022, I decided to reactivate my Match.com subscription. Not exactly sure what that meant. I even happened to remember my password from six months prior. From there, apparently people can begin liking me and send messages. Apparently, I can get some people's messages because they're free like me and others I can't respond to. I responded to the ones I could, and I decided on a lovely foggy New Year's Eve 2022 while sitting home alone with the dog that I was going to pay for my membership. I signed up for another six months because I got a deal, about a third percentage off. My daughter had gone back to where she lived out of state, my son went to a friend's party, I was his DD. I dropped him off, I picked up Chinese carryout, came home, and changed into sweats. That was my evening, and the adventure began.

Religiously, each night, I hit that "Discover" button just to see what's out there. Do I like them, or do I skip them? Or like them and even send a message? Well, I'm not going to divulge my taste all the way. I will admit I'm really not into the "currently separated" guys. Been there, done that, more than I should have and got hurt more than I should have! There are certainly no local men. Local men meaning local men to my county—Harford County, Maryland. I already know the men in this county, and they're all messed up. I probably know them, so we're like siblings, (not West Virginia brother and sister either.) Ha!

I have "discovered" people at least 45 minutes to an hour away, if not upward to an hour and a half in Philadelphia, Pennsylvania or Laurel, Maryland, and any other towns like York, PA and Red Lion, PA. I just keep hitting that Discover button each night. This is what I do. I figured it would take me at least a half hour each night. I've done this religiously every day and today is now January, the 8th. Have not had one date yet. It seems to be that people "like" you as in they hit the Like button, they might say hi, they might write a few sentences, you go back and forth, no one asks you out. Very few men ask for your number. Then, when men do ask for your number, you text back and forth, but there are no phone calls, what happened to that? Am I that old school that we don't talk on the phone first? Where did these basic get-to-know-you questions for dating go? Did I miss something? I mean I'm 53; what happened to saying hi to someone over the phone, hearing the voice, etc.? I don't think I'm old school and too old-fashioned but apparently, I am! So, it goes. I'd rather hear a person's voice first. Maybe it's me? Let me know your thoughts. I am willing to listen and learn.

Not one date yet as of January 8th. Now, keep in mind I knew this would happen. Watch I meet somebody doing something stupid like running to the grocery store, or through a friend of a friend or passively in a bar. I'm a Cancer zodiac sign, a water sign. Summer is my time! Pools, beaches, boats, that's what I'm about. I'm the water lady. I guess that's why I love my hot tub Jacuzzi on my deck so much! Where do I go from here? You hear me not say this once, but many times.

I have a very dear friend, I'll call Marie. It's our joke that the guys I date always come back. In some way, shape, or form, they always do! I run into them somewhere, or they start calling me, or texting after they see me or just out of the blue many months to years later. It's all very weird to me and it's become a joke. I really didn't date this one gentleman that long, but he texts religiously, and I really believe, ladies, and men who read this, the problem we have is timing in life.

Lesson: If the timing is off for either person, it won't work. Then, there is that thing called life. We all have other priorities like our careers, elderly parents, adult children, and even possibly grandchildren. Let's not forget we have to take care of our own home, clean, cook, take of the bills.

For anybody in their 40s and 50s going up to 60s and beyond, this dating sucks! Can I just say it? It does! Let me be truthful about it. How do we get around it? How do we navigate? You know I purposely didn't date too much when I was recently divorced. I wanted to raise my kids, my kids have turned out fantastic so far, and I'm beyond blessed and grateful. I thank God each and every day. I would do it the same way again. Yes, I made parental mistakes. I'm referring to the sacrifice. Where does that leave me? Alone, for now, but hopeful, always hopeful.

Wonderful friends of mine, Gia and Paul, introduced me to a friend of theirs on my 52nd birthday at a local restaurant. They said would you like to meet one of our friends and I'm always up for meeting new gentlemen. I can't say it was a blind date, but basically it was! They told him to come up to where we were celebrating my birthday.

Apparently, they showed him my picture from Facebook, they told him about me, etc. I was just learning of him. I had already eaten, I was dancing, I was a little tipsy, but what the hell? It was my birthday! I meet this guy, Barry; he was really decent-looking. He came up, met my friends, had a blast, and bought us around a shooter or two. My son picked up my girlfriend and me to take us home. This guy even met my son and that was it.

We went out a few times. He was not divorced yet though. He told me his story, while we dated a few times, full disclosure. He was extremely upfront and very honest. You could just tell it wasn't good timing. I could sense it, maybe our energies were off between both of us? Then you wonder when someone texts you every day multiple times, what happened? You think the other person would just know hey this is a bad time for me, I need to regroup. I need a minute. And I fully believe he went back to the girl he was seeing before me. People do it all the time. Yet, what I don't understand is... be honest with the person you went out with.

Lesson: Be honest with the people you date, and, more importantly, be honest with yourself! What are you doing out there? Be upfront.

FAST FORWARD... Here it is, January 11th, and I'm starting to take down Christmas decorations. Who do I hear from? Barry, the guy that I met on my birthday a year and a half ago. He made sure he told me he's divorced now. We shall see. I won't hold my breath though as they say.

It's January 15th, 2023. I had some of my girlfriends over for brunch today that I do annually. I want to say to everyone out there, especially the women, there's nothing like "your tribe." These are the women who stick by you through thick and thin, breakups of guys you're dating, boyfriends you thought you'd end up living together or being married to, deaths, declining parents, even the death of an adult child. You have each other's backs! You celebrate graduations, engagements, marriages, and grandchildren, as well. You are checking on each other during the height of COVID. You drop off Tylenol, food, and drink. This is what we do for each other! We're all divorced, so most of us are alone, empty nesters with only pets. THANK YOU TO MY TRIBE AND YOU KNOW WHO YOU ARE!!

We had seven of us here today with delicious food and the company even better. I made two quiches, one with broccoli and cheese and the other with spinach and mushrooms. I made a few pounds of bacon. Someone brought a hash brown casserole, another brought this breakfast casserole with red peppers, turkey sausage, cheese, and hash browns, we had a French toast casserole too, along with homemade monkey bread. Somebody else brought crepes. It was much needed by all, and a wonderful time was had! I cleaned up and went on my way.

That late afternoon, I had my first meet and greet since signing up with Match for the second time. Let's call this gentleman Tom, shall we say. He was from an area near where I grew up. He too has two children, a boy and a girl and he currently lives in a water town about an hour away. We have been emailing back and forth, then exchanged phone numbers. We had two conversations via text and decided to meet today. Now, let me tell you this. My children, as of this writing, are 23 and 21 almost. I meet a gentleman who is 55 years old, two years older than me, and his children are 18 and 17. The 18-year-old son lives at home with him, and the 17-year-old daughter comes to his home multiple times a week and on his days off which are Thursdays and Sundays. Here is the kicker: he texts me: "I work a lot of weekends and I hope that won't be a problem." That's when I want to go out, Ladies! Especially on the weekend. I can keep myself busy during the week. You work five days a week, workout, run errands, straighten up the house. Who knows if this will work? I was up for the meet and greet, be out of the house, AND just meet someone new.

As of this writing on January 15th, I spent seven weekends at home. Though, I have a full-time job, I also work a part-time nightshift job one night a week. I haven't been going out. Next, he looks a little different from his pictures, he's average. Yes, we have things in common, especially the proximity of where we grew up. We have children of each gender; he's been divorced for years. He's very amicable with his ex and I can't say the same. That's a whole other story! We won't go there. He's a general manager and operating partner of a restaurant. It is not quite a franchise thing, but it's a different venue. He works a lot of weekends. He proceeds to hand me a coupon for a free sandwich at the restaurant. Like that will swoon me and win me over. SMH!! That just made me want him more. NOT! Yet, he did take the time and make the time to meet me. He was very interesting to talk to, I had two beers with him, and he ran into people he used to know through the restaurant industry. He proceeded to have two beers and two shots. He still had a 45-minute drive home I was a little nervous on that, but he said he ate before he met me. That might be a little yellow flag, the drinking, but we shall see.

I get back online and I'm going through things while I'm finding messages that I know are from like three weeks ago. I only paid since

New Year's Eve, how can this be? I guess depending upon the membership or such?

What do we do from here? This is two weeks in, it's my first meet and greet. I'm going to start lining up these dates and each time I'm going to write it down right here. What was that movie? How many first dates? I will keep doing this. I have a few friends who met and have partners because of Match.com. One girlfriend met her husband through POF and they're still going strong. What have I got to lose?

My son, before he returned to college, said, "Mom, we need to find you a boyfriend." LOL. He means well! I do have a lot to offer... Not just my personality of course. I am attractive and I'm not built like Barbie. God did not bless me with that upper chest cavity, if you know what I mean. I am proportionate enough. With going through menopause, I wish the weight would stop at the penthouse and not go to the ground floor if you know what I mean! But I'm still a size 4 all over. THIS IS LIFE. Nobody's perfect at our age! Far, far from it. You know what? I'm a size 4 and I'm working out. For instance, this Sunday, I've worked out three days in a row and I'm off tomorrow for a federal holiday. I will work out again tomorrow and I'm concentrating on my lower abs. There are no rolls on my belly and my obliques are looking good!!

CHAPTER 6

WHAT ARE WE LOOKING FOR AND WHERE?

I was texting with a business associate I worked with years ago, a brilliant man. I'll call him Zach. The most brilliant man I know technically, logically. He was a nuclear physicist in college. He's really someone special to know and he wrote his own fictional books. He reached out via text to say hello. He lives in a different state with his wife even though they have a home here in Maryland as well. I told him I was very down, that I didn't understand God's plan for my life. I say that repeatedly at this age of 53 because I really thought 19 years since my husband left me that there would be a significant other by now. I've been in relationships, but they just didn't work out.

I have been in a few long-term relationships since my divorce. The first was with a functioning alcoholic and I found out the hard way. Another lived an hour away, which wasn't a problem, but all of a sudden, he thought I wanted all this stuff, and I didn't. Then, there was Jaime, that I mentioned previously. Despite his good looks and muscular build, there was not much quality left at the end of the day. Unfortunately, it took me a long time to figure this out. I know he loved me, and he is the one who taught me actions speak louder than words. Yet, he didn't follow his own advice. He promised he was going to get divorced, move in, and give me a ring. I didn't have to be married. Truly I didn't! I'm quite independent and can handle many things. Yet, I was missing a companion, a mate.

Those friends of mine, Gia and Paul, said at that birthday celebration that I would be supporting Jaime. I thought they meant moral support. No, they meant financial support, which is fine and that if someone gets laid off or becomes sick. Yes, I was working two jobs. I basically always have for many years since I got divorced. They stated I would end up supporting him financially as well. I don't need a third child. I love the two I have. I never wanted to raise them solo.

I feel like the longer we date, we know everyone must have emotional baggage. When I say baggage, I don't mean children. They are our blessing. I never want to intrude on somebody and their kids because the kids come first. Now, mine aren't here and when they come home, I want to see them.

The point is... can we find someone we click with, and I don't mean Mr. Right Now, but Mr. Right? Can we find someone who has not only those commonalities or a connection, along with chemistry and sex, as Jonathan Aslay would say? We all want more. Mr. Aslay on YouTube believes most of the world is looking for companionship, chemistry, and sex. That's great, but you need to know if someone wants to commit. I've read a ton of self-help books, especially during COVID, I listened to Jonathan Aslay on video through YouTube. This guy says you can date somebody for a long time and have those things. I really did some introspection. Did I have that with the other gentleman I dated (Jaime)? Is that why the relationship lasted so long? Who knows?

There was chemistry and companionship. I just don't think we were on the same page.

Also, it seems like if you find somebody with all the things you want, then he works weekends or he doesn't work out and stays active. Let me break this down... I would love to find someone who is physically fit, has their children out of the house or darn close to it, loves the beach, boating, to travel, wineries, and festivals. There're some very basic things you can do, like walks to stay active.

Can you find somebody with all the qualities you want? You are lucky if you find 60 to 70% of what you want in a person. That's great! When I say qualities, I should say commonalities or common interests. Let's not forget... you also have to think about morals, values, integrity, religion, and we won't even mention your political stance. I'm very faith-filled. Am I the best Catholic? No. Not even with getting my Catholic annulment. Yet, I also know I couldn't date an atheist or agnostic. Those that say they're religious, or not religious, but spiritual—that's a different story. Think about it—could you be with someone who does not believe in a higher being? For myself, no. Others may find that acceptable. If you are a man who doesn't go to church, OK. If he knows it means that much to you or there's a higher being or just say a prayer, thank the Lord, then that's different.

Lesson: Don't ever, ever give up on what you believe in!

CHAPTER 7

DH

A little more background about me... I thought I married the one. Don't we all say that? He was 18 months older than me, Italian, and I go for those Italian men, ladies! HA! Little on the shorter side for my taste. However, I married the atypical Italian. Can I just say it right here and now?! He was non-affectionate and became worse after we got married. The honeymoon should have been a clue!!! Would you rather take a road adventure tour than be with me, or be with me on the tour and drive a Jeep, then be a little romantic? As I said, he and I were 18 months apart. I usually dated guys a few years older and taller. I think he became very intimidated by me because I was smart, and he didn't like that. He also went along with many topics when he really didn't care, so I found out later.

So, DH was already married and divorced before he and I dated for a year, and then he proposed to me on Christmas evening in front of his entire family. May I say, to all the men out there, getting engaged is a very private thing in my opinion. You don't do that in front of people. It's usually a romantic setting such as dinner, a beach, whatever. More importantly, make it just the two of you. Wherever, you think your bride-to-be will be comfortable.

Lesson: Proposal is not meant to be asked in front of people. Intimacy and privacy are the key.

I accepted, we set a date for our wedding 10 months out. We get married, wait a year, until we start trying to have a family. We have a daughter, then a son. They are two and a half years apart. In May 2003, I was in a major car accident with both children in the car after picking them up from daycare less than three miles from our home. I ended up being medevaced and had to leave both kids on the scene. It was tough!

We go out for a nice birthday dinner for my 34th birthday. He proceeds to tell me over dinner, that he doesn't want to be married anymore. It wasn't like he was drunk, as we each only had one glass of wine with dinner. He pays the bill, we make it to the car, we head home. I proceed to start crying on the ride home. I made it home, paid for the sitter, and went inside. He went for a walk and that was it. You can forget birthday sex!

He came in, slept in the basement for the next three weeks and moved out. I was left with my daughter who was not even four years old, and my son was 18 months. Thus, my marriage of less than six years was over and here I was with two toddlers.

Time goes on. I don't remember that summer because we split ten weeks after I had a major car accident. It was all I could do to get up, go to work, and take care of my two toddlers.

Here we are, nineteen and a half years after we split. He went on to remarry in 2007 to a lovely woman, she changed her major career choice twice, she had three children from a prior marriage. They merge households and buy a large house. That lasted about six years and she left him, they divorced.

Then, my ex meets someone else at work apparently. She moves in, she has her kids 50% of the time. He proposes and they get married in June of 2017. They stay married for a few years. In the middle of COVID in October 2021, she leaves him. That's right, can you do the math? Are you keeping score? He's been married four times and divorced four times!!

You see, there is a pattern. My ex is nice, I fell in love with him, he has many good qualities. He can be thoughtful, kind, funny, he is smart, and has a good personality. Yet all that can change in the blink of an eye. When he would come home after work, I didn't know who was walking through that door. Was it Jekyll or was it Hyde? He could switch personalities at the drop of a dime. Nothing was ever good enough. I couldn't fold the towels correctly and one day, he pulled them out from the master bathroom closet. They sat on the floor for two days until I folded them. He has some issues. It is called being bi-polar.

I will probably take a quarter to a third of the responsibility for the marriage failing. Yet, it takes two people with some real effort. Of course, everybody can say it's only one side of the story. There are three sides: his side, her side, and the truth!

You see, after our divorce, he did go to therapy and took antidepressants. He did it after the third wife and the fourth wife. However, sometimes you need therapy longer than a few months. We all have to do introspection and work on ourselves. It takes some deep diving. He chose not to do that after a few months. He would do a little therapy, go on medication and everything was fine. He meets someone new they would date, he would stop therapy, and stop the medication. After a few years, the cycle starts all over again. There you have it.

CHAPTER 8

ONTO JANUARY

It's January 17th, 2023, and each night, I hit that 'Discover' button. Who's out there waiting for me? Are they from New Jersey? That's a bit too far from Maryland. You can make it to Camden, NJ, in about an hour and a half to two hours, but do I want a relationship with a partner that far? Would you, ladies? Some people don't mind long-distance relationships.

Let's think about it... And it all depends on where you are in life. How far is too far to go to meet someone or to begin a relationship, possibly even the love of your life? I'm not saying East Coast to West Coast or Midwest. But within reason. What is a decent drive? An hour? An hour and a half? Two hours? I was googling maps before I hit like because of some towns I've never heard of in Pennsylvania, and quite frankly, Maryland also.

Some southern towns could be like two hours away and this one guy wrote that he was from Frederick. Previously, I dated a guy from Frederick, and it is about an hour and 10 minutes away, which is doable. Then, when we were messaging, he mentioned he was from Poolesville. That town is further than Frederick, but he said nobody recognizes that town and that's like an hour 45 minutes from my address. I have another guy who seems nice, we have a lot in common from Mechanicsville, MD. Has anyone out there heard of it? Of course, I've heard of it. But where exactly is it? I don't know! Again, it's like an hour and 45 minutes away.

Here's another question to ponder... How about what kind of status are you willing to date a man? Meaning divorce? Currently separated? Or never married? Let me give you my take because I do have a few years' experience on this. Now, that's a laugh and a half right there. Since I have been divorced for 18 years, I have attempted to date a bit.

Divorced, that's quite acceptable! However, you have to make sure they're over their divorce and not dwelling on it! You have the currently separated. That's fine if you want a companion, a buddy to do things with. Even if you want to be FWBs, who am I to say? Maybe it's for the season, but not for the reason. Or maybe he could be your Mr. Right Now, as you both grow through that season, but he's not Mr. Right! The problem with the currently separated status is that I have been promised too many things that never came to fruition, and I've been hurt too many times as in the case with Jaime.

How about the guys who have never been married? Is that good or bad? The pro could be: they don't have emotional baggage (from a marriage, I mean) or some people view children as baggage. I do not!! I think it's terrible to refer to children as baggage. Yet, do they always want to party? They've just been too selfish? They truly haven't met the right one? They don't want to commit? An empty nester, who likes to travel, could meet someone and they don't have to get married in the future. Or does it mean, something's really wrong with them and there is a reason why they've never been married? Just the thought to ponder. And where do you go from here? Oh, but wait, let's not forget the widowers. That brings a whole new status into the game.

The last time I signed up for Match.com, which was January through June of 2022, I dated a widower. Mitch was a widower with three grown children, two adult daughters and one adult autistic son. The one adult daughter was married, the other adult daughter was living with her boyfriend, and the adult autistic son lived with him. Mitch was a really nice guy, a gentleman, polite, and kind. Yet, he was newly widowed as his wife hadn't been deceased for a year. She died during COVID, but not because of COVID. An aneurysm was the cause of her death. My point is... no one can say it's a certain amount of time to grieve, but they were together 30 something years. He's out there dating, taking me to dinners, and we meet in a public place. We had some wonderful dinners and that was it. We would have a two-hour dinner, we would talk, catch up, and go our separate ways. He was funny, respectable, and nice-looking. He cancelled on me once because of the weather as it was extremely cold and windy. I guess we went out about a half dozen times and had some wonderful meals together. Then, he cancelled on me the second time at like 3:00 o'clock for 6:30 p.m date. He never followed up to go out again. There you have it!

Lesson: Gentlemen don't cancel with the same lady twice unless it is a really good reason like a true emergency. The weather or not up to it does not qualify. And ladies, if a guy cancels on you twice without a proper reason, perhaps he is not that interested.

I'll leave you with those thoughts to ponder. Which status of a man is best to date, and ultimately, to have a long-term relationship with? Is it divorced, and then you have to think about how many times he's been divorced? Is currently separated any better? Never married and where is that going to go? And I might say when I hit that 'Discover; button, I'm absolutely astounded by the number of people who were never married, but they have kids, just saying. Lastly, are the widows of the world really ready or do they just want a dinner companion?

On January 18th, I have my second meet and greet. This is the second one in four days. We're going to meet up at a local almost sports bar that has good food. He did offer to come up this way, he lives about 30 minutes away, we have some things in common; we talked prior, and thought we shall see where it goes. He has 28-year-old fraternal twin sons, and his name is Rich.

Here it goes... let me fill you in on Rich's story. He proceeds to tell me about his career, what he does, where he works. That's all part of the first encounter, you know, the meet and greet. Then, he proceeds to tell me about his sons. One lives about an hour away, owns his own home, and his girlfriend lives with him, and he works on a cannabis farm. He does quite well for himself financially. The other son is not quite the same. He and his wife enabled him. He is away in a halfway house many states away. He says he's been revived a few times with Narcan, and he has stopped giving him money for years. This really saddened me because I hate to hear that about anyone's relative in this regard.

He goes on to tell me that he hopes to retire by October 2023 and take his boat to Key West. He recently spent 14 weeks there, staying with a friend, vacationing, sightseeing, getting to know the area. I felt like saying, why are you on a dating site? Am I the bad one here? The more he is talking, I'm thinking we can go out and have fun, enjoy a meal, some laughs, and listen to his stories. However, I really want a relationship, I am not ready to sell my house and move.

Just when I think maybe I will give him a chance, it's not certain he's going retire in October, we shall see, he proceeds to tell me more.

Rich states that he hasn't been in a relationship in about two years. I understand, that happens. We take breaks from dating, our careers are more demanding, and then there was a little thing called COVID. The world was a mess. I shake my head and nod. He says he was with a woman for a total of six years; she moved in with him after about a year. They started an eBay business together and she wanted to control things. She's a nurse, she wanted a "Mommy Makeover." I'm looking at him like this is crazy. I keep my mouth shut, which can be hard for me to do! This woman goes to Mexico to have this done. While she was there, her stomach perforated from the bariatric surgery, she had done prior. She ends up in a hospital in Mexico, the cartel is holding her hostage there; she wants him to get her out of the country, so he pays to have her ticket changed. He picks her up from the airport, and takes her right to the hospital; they're trying to understand why she is so sick, and her kidneys are shutting down. She ends up having bone cancer and this woman is in her mid-4os. I'm thinking this poor nurse, this woman doesn't seem too bright to me. OK she has bariatric surgery done. I get it. But apparently, doesn't know her own body that something's wrong. Then, you have to go to a foreign country to get this mommy makeover? Who really is doing this? Is she half-sane or what? You cannot truly make this stuff up!! Hence, writing a book.

Forget that they have broken up and she has a teenage daughter. Apparently, she's trying to move out of HIS house. Since she found out she had cancer, he told her she could stay in **his** house that he owns, and which her name was not on. He lives on his boat at a local yacht club WITH his German Shepherd on the boat. Say it with me this time... are you freaking kidding me? Unbelievable. Can I say OMFG?!

My former husband up and left me with two toddlers, I bought him out of our marital home. Most men give it to the wives/mothers of their children. In the meantime, I did enjoy myself. He walked me to my car, we hugged goodbye, that was it. Definitely won't meet him again!

He let me know he was home, walking his dog, had a great night, blah blah blah. Match apparently automatically renewed his subscription, but he did not want that. I told him how to turn it off, he thanked me, and says he's glad he got a chance to meet me. So where does that leave dating, ladies? What's a woman to do? I don't get it. We shall see.

I come home after this two-hour diversion, let the dog out, eat a little something else. I had two beers, and he and I split a pound of shrimp that were very good from our local county establishment. Some conversation, chilled out, heard stories, and I realized my life is pretty good!

Seriously though, I'm lonely. I had a 2-hour outing tonight with this meet and greet. Then, home to the dog, watching Netflix, reading a book, whatever.

While I realize this Match subscription is a diversion, I'm still lonely. I've been on it for three weeks, and I've had two meet-and-greets. This other guy from Annapolis wants to meet again, but I don't know when or where. The kicker with him is... he has his kids, and yes, they're older but still...

On January 19th, after running an errand after work, making dinner, and changing clothes. I settled in to look at my Match account. What do I find? Nine messages from men. Let's go through them one by one. A few were really far away; I recognize that with a few, the hobbies weren't even aligned. UGH!!

You read and re-read with the likes, dislikes, their little bio, you keep paging down and then it states... atheist. No, I don't think so. I proceed to write people back and one guy who thought I ignored him, even though I didn't know where his message popped up, starts generating lots of messages via Match. His name is John; he and I exchange numbers and we continue to text a lot into the night. I mean like hours. Yet, he won't hit the green button with the phone symbol a.k.a. the SEND call button. Men don't want to hear a person's voice and it just amazes me!!! How can we not hear another person's voice? The inflection, the general respect, and mutual interest conveyed between two adults. I don't get it!!! We're texting back and forth which is OK, but a phone call is so much quicker, saves time, you can tell if they talk like Mickey Mouse, etc. Really nice guy it seems. He's super built—muscular with six-pack abs. He offered to let me come to his gym and offered to train me at the gym. I told him I'm working on my abs and doing these YouTube videos. Yet, going through menopause, it's a bit hard to get your abdominal area cut. He proceeds to tell me to watch the dairy and sugar because they're the worst thing for the abs. You can keep doing them, but the sugar and dairy intake cannot get one the abs. He works out about five times a week. That's a little bit too much for me, but he is a text buddy, right? I have to look at it that way. LOL, I will look at a guy's cut eight-pack any day! I am still human and not dead!!

Some of the guys like to ask all these questions like it's an interview. What's your favorite hobby and why? How did that become your favorite hobby? How passionate are you about that hobby? What drives you to do that? Really? A freaking hobby? Another guy wanted to know my favorite trail. Seriously, this is the best we can do?? Oh, another golden question...what's your favorite color? Really?

Should I tell these gentlemen that I have spent all these years raising kids by myself? I got my career in alignment. I'll share more about that later. It's not easy to raise two kids, run them to their sports and activities, maintain a home, pay the bills, clean it, cook, and everything else. I'm just re-discovering my hobbies, if you will. I don't want to hear that I'm boring or that I just take hikes, or I don't work out enough. It seems that you have these men who are working out five days a week, like John, who is 61 and in spectacular shape. The alternative is a few extra pounds, and they don't care about anything. Now, let me tell you... their interpretation of a few extra pounds and my interpretation of a few extra pounds is a few extra pounds different!! Really?! Can I find something in between? Am I this picky? I think not. I'm not obsessed with being in shape, and unfortunately, I probably snack too much. There you have it.

On January 20th, I wake up to another seven messages and a reply to these gentlemen. You just keep doing this back and forth. It's like an electronic password via e-mail and messages. It's not that I'm not getting likes and people sending me messages, but you have to go back and forth. You e-mail a little bit, then you exchange numbers, or they offer theirs. Here we are. I would much rather talk on the phone, or meet in person.

Then, I had this person, Gino, and he works downtown at a hospital, and I'm guessing he lives downtown because he recommended a very nice restaurant downtown, really the bar. However, he suggested a time which is late. I offered a time right after work. He does not know that I work a second job that night, on the night shift here and there. Nonetheless going downtown, paying for parking, and he's not offering to meet me up here or even halfway, nothing. He suggested a Saturday night and it was last minute, didn't give a day's notice and I had plans. He proposed a Friday but I was not driving down there on Friday at 8:00 p.m. I said right after work thinking like 5:30 or 6. He works late most nights. So how can you do that? These people get on there and how can they attempt to date with the work schedules? Yes, I'm bad on a Friday night, but no one's mentioning during the week; it's like you can only go out on a weekend night. Sometimes, you have more fun on a weeknight.

I like doing things during the week; it breaks it up even if you meet at 6 to 8 p.m. It's something to do during the week.

I'm supposed to meet Tom, the gentleman from the waterfront town, that has children or at least one living with him and sees the other one on Sunday. We're going to meet at 3:00 p.m. on Sunday; he's going to drive toward my area and do most of the driving, which I feel bad about (and don't). I offered to meet him at least halfway toward his side through the Baltimore tunnel and we'll see. Between you and me, it'll be like two hours, it'll be over which is fine because he'll go back to his kids. Not that I think you should state all this when on the bio of your dating profile, but you should say you have a job where you primarily work weekends. Your point would be to find another person in that business, or they work those hours. More to follow.

On Saturday, I was supposed to casually meet someone for dinner, Cameron. He lives close less than 20 minutes from me, is few years younger, we never exchanged numbers. Instead, he suggested grabbing a casual bite to eat over e-mail for Saturday evening. Now, there you go. Sounds like a plan to me. Let's do it. Waiting for further confirmation to go on, and that will be that.

I have another gentleman, Sam, who is about 5o minutes from me, we exchanged e-mails, talked on the phone, and he has a wonderful sense of humor. We are getting together on Monday. That's three lined up in three days! Now, we're talking!

I meet Cameron at a local restaurant who is meet and greet number three. He's dressed nice in a button-down shirt with a nice Polo sweater over it. He is mostly bald, shaved his head, kind of a big guy. We are seated at a booth in the restaurant, we're talking, he does not drink alcohol, good conversation, he's a heavy equipment operator. I'm not judging. It's just different because I am more educated and, with my career, it would help keep the conversation going. Who doesn't enjoy a good conversation? I enjoy a sense of humor even more so!!!

We managed to talk about marriages, kids, travel. The meal took a little bit longer than usual, just for sandwiches. I really thought the evening was going well. It was approaching about two hours, then the check comes. As I always do, I offer to split it or even tip.

Cameron responds to me, "Let me ask you a question."

I reply, "OK."

He says, "Would you be interested in seeing me again?"

"Yes, we can do that," I tell him.

His reply was you can pick up the next bill. Now, ladies, not that I wouldn't have offered. It's the point of it! Is it me? Shouldn't he have just saved it for the next time or said would you be interested in getting together again? Then, he waits til I offer? Have to tell you, I was a little put off by that. He then walks me to my car, gives me a hug, and we part ways. Three days later, he calls me, and he asks me out for Saturday, and I happen to have plans to go to a Bull and Oyster Roast, which I have had for months.

On Sunday, it's time to meet up with Tom. He comes up from the water town and we meet at a local sports bar, he beats me there, ordered an appetizer, and had a beer waiting. How thoughtful! It was a rainy, cold Sunday and I have a turtleneck sweater on. I can't get warm;

I really should have canceled the date. Yet remember, Sundays are his best days to get together!!

We watch a playoff game and we're talking. He proceeds to tell me he wants to hit the place where we met the first time on his way home to take home more Greek salad and shrimp salad. I respond with an OK. He then suggested at halftime, we leave the sports bar where we were, and go to that original place. We do that. We recognize people from the previous week, or at least I do. He doesn't remember meeting them. He has two beers to my one beer. He receives his order, game is over, and we leave.

Let me set the stage for what's about to happen next. This little restaurant/bar is in a shopping center. He is parked in front and I'm on the side. He offered to walk me to my car, but it was cold, and the wind was blowing the rain. I said, no, it's OK, we hugged, gave a peck on the cheek and went on our way. He was going to text me when he got home. I run a quick errand in the area, head home, and get gas on the way. He texts he was home, and if I wanted to get together again, text or call. Obviously, I sensed something was up.

I reply I enjoyed the time today and getting to know you. Not sure what you meant? He goes on to say, "I really thought you'd kiss me more; I really enjoy kissing. I'm not into dating many people, I'm really attracted to you." BLAH BLAH BLAH. Are you freaking kidding me again? I set the stage as to the place where we were parting. Now, let me mention to you, his attire. We know how the weather was, we know it's our second time being around one another, he shows up in a really nice navy hoodie, a baseball cap, a very casual outfit. That's fine! It's Sunday for a game. May I also add that he had a 5 o'clock shadow? Wait, it was more like a 10 o'clock shadow. Really? How old are we? We're not 16 or 18! What are we supposed to do? Sit in the car and make out like we're those ages? Are you freaking kidding me?

I was not going to get into a text battle with him. He proceeded to text me three more messages saying how attractive I am, how he is attracted to me, it was like we had two dates in a very public setting, everybody talking about the game. This is like yellow/orange flags being waved right here. My radar is going off. I mean my mind is racing like the Indy 500. Two dates and you want to make out in a very public place in the rain? I don't know you, dude.

Don't get me wrong—I can be romantic, and the rain can be also. You are the one rushing home to your kids and can only meet on a Sunday!

On Monday, I meet Sam at a place about 40 minutes from him and 30 minutes from me. Normally, Monday is the night that I attend a non-denominational church in the area. Sometimes, you have to break that pattern. I will watch the church service online!

Nonetheless, this guy really wanted to meet because he was going out of town for work and transitioning jobs. Keep in mind we had talked twice on the phone prior to the meeting. He called on Saturday and Sunday. Now, there is a guy that knows how to hit that green send button. Each time we talked was at least 30 minutes. He has a great sense of humor, we laughed the phone, I looked forward to meeting him. We have a nice meal, nothing fancy, one beverage of alcohol. We were there for about two hours; he is really funny. He walked me to my car, gave me a hug. On the phone, he told me he would pick up the bill. I, said well, we can split it. He said no I'm chivalrous, I will handle the bill. I started to and he just shook his head at dinner and that was it. He texted me when he got home, I did the same. We spoke the following night, Tuesday, for an hour and 50 minutes. We're trying to get together again by the end of the week. However, I have plans for the upcoming weekend, he's transitioning jobs, and he needs training out of town. He has to pack one day and leave on Sunday. He is staying in touch. He was meet and greet number four. Slowly, I am getting some dates. Isn't this fun? I have many other words to describe... fun is not one!

CHAPTER 9

JANUARY ENDS

By Wednesday, January 25th, 2023, I had two of these gentlemen ask me out for the upcoming Saturday night, January 28th, 2023. I already have plans for a bull and oyster roast in the area as a fundraiser that my cousins who started a 501 C corporation and it's like a mini-reunion. Cameron, the gentleman from the casual dinner who said I could pay for the next day, ask me out. Also, John, the guy who works out, just texts, but never calls. Ladies, this is feast or famine as usual!! How can this be? Is Saturday night the only night to have a date night? Are the stars only allowing us to get to know someone new on that magical night or does TV just suck that much that we rather be out with another single, heterosexual person of the opposite sex? Just saying!

Lesson: Gentlemen, I have said it before, and I will say it again. There are seven days a week. Life happens more than just on Saturdays. Just saying!!

On Friday, January 27th, I had my second date with Samuel, and again, we met at the same restaurant as prior. The same place we ate the first time four days prior. I go there right after work, traffic was much heavier, so we sit there and talk and order dinner. Great conversation as usual, the meal was good, and the company, better. I will note, he did get a haircut and it looked great on him. However, he wore the same outfit. Jeans fine, shoes fine. It's a pullover, but I saw him in the same one a few days ago. I thought he would put something different on? Maybe I'm being a witch? Am I being too picky? Is it me, Ladies?

He is in a training program for the next two weeks for this new job as he's changing types of industries, he did call the next day as he said he would. He has asked me once Friday night at the end of the date, and then again on Saturday over the phone if I am interested in him. Not sure what to do about this? I ate another healthy meal of tuna, a different dish from the prior night. He walked me to my car, and I gave him a ride to his. He was very respectable, gave me a hug and a kiss and we were both on our way. He called me on his way home since he hit traffic. We shall see.

It's the end of January 2023. Has everybody kept score of this lovely story? How many men have I met in the month of January 2023? Well... I've met four. One month down of my Match subscription and five more to go!! Can one really find the relationship they want, and a person that checks all the boxes, as one girlfriend says? Are two people willing to compromise? What side of town they live on? Or travel plans? Merging lives together?

It's 2023, bring it on! It's going to be my year! Why? I am going to take care of myself for once! I've been an empty nester for two and a half years now, made it through the pandemic by myself, and it's all about me! I'm setting more and more boundaries, demanding respect, **and I not settling for less.** It's got to be a two-way street and people have to do something for me. Just saying. Does that sound like a BITCH? Perhaps, but I don't think so. It's healthy, no more co-dependent crap, no more dysfunctionality. NO MORE! Let's be direct in a nice way, and onward. It's all about ME!! LET'S DO THIS!!

CHAPTER 10

NELLIE

I have a very, a very dear friend named Nellie. She's extremely intelligent, attractive, thin, kind, and has a wonderful personality. She is retired Air Force; now, a teacher with her PhD and assistant principal. She has been through hell and back—what most people haven't in a lifetime. I won't go into intimate details, but this woman is the epitome of strength, courage, and faith.

Let me share some of her dating experiences. These are worth a laugh and a half and more! I do have her permission to share these. I will name a few instances of what it is like for both men and women dating in our 5os. This is no lie!! This is what it's like. It's not always fun, certainly not! We put ourselves out there; we try to meet someone to eventually be in a long-term relationship.

She had a date set up at a nice restaurant. It was not a four-star, but it was better than a very casual dining place. She met the man, they're at the dinner table looking at menu, and his hands are deformed like lobster claws. He could barely hold the menu. His table manners were atrocious. Quite frankly, it kind of freaked her out. She did not know what to make of it. She was being polite. They ordered, dined, and finished their conversation. He didn't explain anything to her, and he acted like everything was normal when he could barely hold his utensils as well. His hands were like claws. What should she do? Say something or not? She was quite uncomfortable and awkward. What would you do?

Lesson: For both men and women: if you do not feel comfortable putting this kind of information on your online profile, then at least tell the person. You don't want to disclose over e-mail or the phone, ok. Tell the person when you see them.

For her second dating experience, she had been communicating with a man, they emailed, texted, and spoke on the phone. They got to know each other a bit. A date, time and day have been arranged. The day before the date, the man texts her and says he's not going go out on anymore dates. He's going to stay at home with his pug dogs and they are his doppelgangers. Are you freaking kidding me? Just say, we're not a match, there is nothing in common. Instead, you say you'd rather stay home with your pug dogs and they're your doppelgangers!! What have we come to as adults in dating? Just be honest, but gentle.

Lesson: Every time there is a shred of hope that things might be going well, don't count on it. You never know what happens at all.

Let me explain a third dating experience of my girlfriend, Nellie. Again, e-mails were exchanged; then, telephone numbers exchanged, conversations and texts took place. A gentleman suggested they meet at a very fine dining restaurant, a four-star restaurant. He even brought her a dozen red roses and mentioned they could tell their grandchildren they met there on their first date. They would tell them that's where they met! Isn't that sweet? Isn't that romantic? The meal was delicious, and the company was even more enjoyable! Dinner ended, they hugged, kissed, said their goodbyes, and that was it. Guess what? She never heard from him again. Isn't that something? Why do men say this nonsense? It's ridiculous! What is the point? Was he sincere? Did he get cold feet? I mean it seems you have those experiences or the 'let's meet for a cup of coffee' and there is nothing in between.

Lesson: Men, why do you do this? Make a woman feel like a queen for a few hours, put her on a pedestal and disappear like Superman? The abundance and charm are not needed.

Nellie was on the same dating site I am on now, Match.com. About this time a year ago, we were both on the site. It was April of 2022; I had met someone, and she had also. They had about ten dates and were going along. My date and I had only about six dates, but we talked for hours on the phone since we lived an hour apart. She and her date, Alan, met up with me and my date. We had a great conversation among the four of us, laughed, and the two couples danced. I was very impressed with her date, Alan! Later, I found out my date was as well.

About a week later, I hear her date told her why can't we be like so and so and her date meaning me and my date? I busted out laughing immediately. I said Nellie, did you tell him that the guy I am seeing, and I talk every night on the phone for at least an hour? That's a huge difference and we've built up this rapport, we laugh, tease one another. Another week goes by, she and Alan are speaking on the phone. He tells her he just wants to take her and live in a bubble with no one else. While I can understand the sentiment to a point, it's kind of creepy! Who wants to live in a bubble? We were still in COVID; didn't we just live in a bubble? Who wants to do that again with a person they barely know? That's unhealthy! And, to use the analogy of a bubble. HMMM, what do you think of that? I believe it was a compliment. It seemed a little strong though.

Lesson: Perhaps, we (both men and women) interpret certain sentiments in the wrong way intended? However, be aware of what you say to the person you are starting to see. I am all for being open, honest, and direct. Yet, being in a bubble leaves something to be desired.

Here's the fifth example of dating online and this is what we must look out for, especially women. Nellie was conversing with a man via e-mails back and forth and she got the funny feeling something wasn't right. Was it intuition? Was it instinct? Something was off. She got his last name. She proceeded to look him up on Facebook and what did she find? When she clicked on him, his status stated he was married. She was flabbergasted, embarrassed, and in disbelief. She proceeded to take a snapshot of his Match.com dating profile and instantly messaged his wife. She found her through the guy's Facebook profile. She explained that she was on Match.com, they had been conversing as the husband stated he was single. She wrote a message to the wife stating she was not a homewrecker, she believed in the sanctity of marriage, and she never would interrupt the institution of marriage. Nellie is a very faithful woman who believes in the commitment of a relationship.

Lesson: Ladies, always trust your intuition and instinct. When something seems amiss, it usually is. That goes for men also when querying about the lady you are dating. Perhaps, we (both men and women) interpret certain sentiments. Always be alert and cautious.

One last interesting story that Nellie relayed to me. She had a friend who started seeing someone from a dating site. They were not dating that long, still getting to know one another. They meet at a restaurant and sit in a booth. He wanted her to sit on the same side of the booth as he, as opposed to across from him. She does that. They are looking at the menu and ordered drinks. They ordered their meal and are talking. All of the sudden, the woman feels like his whole head on her shoulder. She is nudging him to stop, elbowing him, but could not get him to move. She realized he is unconscious. She calls for help, the staff dials 911. The restaurant employees continue to try to wake him up. His date reaches for his cell phone to call someone. She recognizes someone with the same last name, hoping it is his daughter. She calls the number, introduces herself as so and so's date and that it seems he had an instant heart attack. The woman on the phone responds, "Good. He deserves it. Good luck." It turns out it was his ex-wife.

The date was so flustered after the incident and calling the former spouse, who had such a reaction. She swore off dating, especially online dating. She would rather be by herself than go through this. Just imagine, ladies—you just ordered your meal, having conversation and your date keels over. His last words were probably, "I would like Parmesan on my salad." If I were her, I would swear off online dating also. Can it get any worse?

Lesson: While online dating, be prepared for anything and I do mean ANYTHING!!!

Let me tell you two stories my two different girlfriends relayed to me about their second dates. They met these men online. Notice I didn't say 'gentlemen'?!

My girlfriend explained to me that she met this guy on Bumble—the dating app where the women swipe and choose the men, for those not familiar. This dating app seemed to be working for her. A guy friend of mine said to me I don't like that app because the women have all the control. Can we say yellow flag right there? I looked at him and I went, ohhhhh really? Does that explain why he's going after women 20-plus years younger than he? I said you do realize you could be their father? Ha!

Back to the point... She had a date with this guy from Richmond, Virginia. She goes there to visit a relative. They had a wonderful first date. Fantastic dinner, great company, it was a few hours long. They discussed many things. They have been emailing and having phone conversations up to this point. On the second date, they proceed to an Italian restaurant. Let me set the stage as she did in relaying the story. The restaurant is quaint with a lovely atmosphere and it's very romantic with a little candle on the table. She has a glass of wine. I'm setting the scene here folks. She ordered some type of lobster tortellini. She is very thin, in shape, she really wanted to enjoy this delicious entrée.

He proceeds to tell her on the second date that he's impotent. She is saying this to me over a phone conversation and says, are you there? Are you there? I said, I am indeed! She says, you went quiet the way I did! LOL. She says, I almost choked on my pasta. I had to ask, what did you do? She just shook her head and swallowed her food. He proceeds to tell her this because he wants to be honest. I told her I understand that. I am all for honesty, folks. Nothing beats it. Can I say there may be a however? There is a time and place.

He proceeds to explain he hasn't had vaginal sex since 2016. He goes on to say that other things worked on his anatomy, and he could take care of a female in other ways. Then he proceeded to name them. Keep in mind—this is a second date. I am thinking you haven't discovered if you even want to do it with this guy. Or maybe you are thinking that, but do you have to reveal this knowledge during dinner? Just saying.

Gentlemen, there is honesty and I'm 122% for honesty and, straightforwardness, being direct and transparent. I am the queen of that!! Let me just give you a clue here... it was the second date!! You don't even know if you have enough to converse together, short of a one-night stand or you know you want something casual, why disclose this? So soon I mean!! I believe in honesty. I truly do. I suppose he didn't want to waste her time, but by the same token, did you really need to say it then and there? In the middle of a wonderful meal, she's dressed in a lovely little black dress (LBD).

I was just astounded, and she was supposed to go back and meet him in another month. She ended up telling him that she decided not to make the trip, she had to cancel it since something came up. I inquired, why weren't you honest with him?

The former person I was... would have done what she did. I would have just said I don't think it's a good match and not for that reason. I would have said you said it way too soon and I don't even know if I even want to have sex with you so soon!! Are you really freaking kidding me?

That girl has another girlfriend who I have not met, but I've heard a lot about. She thought she met a really nice gentleman, if you want to call them that?!! They had a great first date, went out to dinner, and talked a lot in between emails. For the second date, he suggested a picnic. That is kind of a cool, unique idea. No pressure, getting to know one another, creative, but little effort went into it. Just something different! I said, as long as, it wasn't hot or too cold or rainy. What a fabulous idea!!

She proceeds to meet him in this park, so they're in a public location. He brought sandwiches and something to drink, some fruit. He also brought a lovely little wrapped box! Every lady likes a little gift once in a while!! Or maybe not... as you say in the best Keith Morrison Dateline voice!

This box is small, beautifully wrapped, very ornate lovely bow. She couldn't believe it. It was the second date. Why would he bring her a gift so soon? He proceeds to tell her it could be dessert! Interesting. The girlfriend, relaying the story, proceeds to ask me what do you think it is? I reply, gee, I don't know... maybe a beautiful cupcake that's very ornately decorated? Or a small little dessert they could share, like a little fruit tart or mini cheesecake or something of that nature?

She said OK and she's repeating the whole story about how it's beautifully decorated, it's small, and he's going on and on and he wants her to open it before they even eat! I said, well that's a little odd. She says what do you think it is now? I reply now, you have me thinking. I think it's like a pair of thongs or a small teddy or something like that. I really thought it was a pair of lace underwear or something. Are you ready for this one? LOL!

My girlfriend proceeds to tell me that her friend opened this lovely gift, and it was a sexual toy that you strap on. He says to her maybe we can have fun with this?!

Are you f*##%^ kidding me? Mind you, let me repeat myself... this is the second date!! I was stunned. I was married for just short of six years and my boring ex-husband never even brought that up. I've been in relationships since. You may talk about it the older you get for a little help. But really? The second date? TMI TMI!!

Lesson: To all the men out there—first, do not disclose your sexual status as being impotent on the second date. Truly, make sure it's a person you want to have sex with, and they feel the same! Suppose you disclose that, and the person never wanted to have sex with you anyway? Just saying.

Second, as there are two lessons in this chapter, men do not go buying sexual toys for a person for the second date. Can I say that qualifies AFTER the first few months. UNLESS, you and the individual have already disclosed that and have no problem with it!!

CHAPTER 11

OBSERVATIONS

Girlfriends and I discuss what are each other's types of men to date. Not sure I have one. However, I have dated more blue-collar type workers than other friends. Although I not only have my bachelor's degree, I have my master's degree and my PMP certification. Regardless, I know many men and have dated men who do not have degrees. That does not bother me. They can be respectful, sincere, and stay in shape. However, as the girlfriends and I spoke, they explained to me why they choose not to date blue-collar workers. It seems as if the blue-collar workers are not as emotionally intelligent. Is that always true? I don't believe so. I think that's a generalization we all make in life. You cannot rule out every blue-collar worker, not today or ever. Just because he doesn't have degrees, he can be emotionally intelligent. The majority of them seem to not be emotionally intelligent, however. Now, I get it.

Case in point is William, who was previously described. He had great qualities, but he never wanted to talk about anything. His communication skills were lacking. How do you get to know a person? What do they want to do in the future? Anything at all? You have to open up to your partner. The more I said, can we talk a little during dinner, he would shut me out. He'd rather sit there and play Keno. It was me or watching the random numbers pop up. I saw how unmportant I was, and I'd rather be alone!!! I have better company solo.

Lesson: I don't care who you are, what you do, always find company within yourself. Be able to be alone. I know I can!

As we all know, communication is vital in any relationship. It doesn't have to be solely with a significant other, with the child, parent, or friends. We all must talk and tell each other how we feel if we're going to get anywhere in life. With a significant other especially, you have to talk about the future and what you both want. One may want to stay local when they retire, be a homebody and not travel. The other may want to travel, or even move to a warmer state. You have to figure all this out and discuss things.

I was watching this movie on Netflix called Love in the Villa. It was about a third-grade teacher who saved up for this trip for many years to go to Verona, Italy. She looked forward to it, she thought her boyfriend of many years would accompany her. Right before she is bound to leave for the trip, he breaks up with her. She decides to go on the trip solo. She had a villa rented like an Airbnb and it was already rented out to a man. A young, good-looking British man who let her sleep on the sofa. As the story develops, she is trying to push him out of the Airbnb. It got ugly for a few scenes. They were quite mean to each other.

Slowly, they realized they had more in common. They both love Shakespeare and in particular Romeo and Juliet. They recited the lines to each other, they talked about the villa where they stayed, they talked about statues. They were discussing their upbringing and their parents. He had guessed that her boyfriend had broken up with her right before she went on this trip. He asks her you're not going to get back with your ex, are you? He goes on to say, "Getting back with your ex is like putting on dirty underwear after you get out of the shower."

I literally laughed out loud when I heard this. Very clever indeed! This was a major point, and I can certainly understand it. Just a thought to ponder. I really recommend the movie as well on Netflix.

Lesson: the quote about getting together with your ex. They are an ex for a reason, especially if they did you dirty. If it's like someone is confused and you can tell, it doesn't make it any easier. This example really makes you think.

Another scene in the movie was when they were both talking about their parents. She said her parents couldn't keep their hands off one another. She felt it was embarrassing. He was talking about his parents' relationship, which was almost the opposite. She asked why didn't one of his parents leave the other. His response was, "Power in a relationship is the one who cares the less." Isn't that interesting? That summed it up!! I know many couples where one partner does more over and over and over for the other partner and everybody's happy. I am not sure what I'm doing wrong to have not achieved that in any relationships I have had. More thoughts to ponder.

Lesson: For myself going forward, I am going to care a lot less. When you do that, I have observed, things falls into place.

CHAPTER 12

FEBRUARY 2023

January rolled into February and here we are! Though January is a long month filled with many responsibilities, I managed to meet three gentlemen. Two of these men, I had dates with each. It's the beginning of February, and I bet you I have five gentlemen e-mailing me nightly. Now, that may not seem like many to any of you. However, working a full-time job as I do in management, working a part-time night shift job as I do one night a week, still taking care of the house, and a dog, this is a job in itself. Just trying to find a man! Lol. Every night I hit that discover button religiously. What is out there? More important, who is out there? Are the pictures true to the individual? Did they write a little blurb or not? You really have to look at all this to nail it down.

Each night, I return messages of men back and forth. Prior to that, I look at the "likes" and see if there are any messages there worth returning. It's all behind a screen and keyboard. Can I just ask why, in this day and age, we only text? I really need to know this. Feel free to reach out and tell me. Why are we hiding behind the phone and text only? That goes for men and women both! How can I hear your voice? Is it sexy, is it deep and DJ-like? I'd like to hear someone's voice. You get a feel for them. I went on a meet and greet years ago, we didn't talk on the phone prior to meeting, only texts and e-mails. I meet this person and I felt like he was talking to a squirrel. It was like one of those animations like real squeaky animal. Picture this, ladies, like shut your eyes and picture a squirrel cartoon character and he's chipping away at his acorn or a nut. Needless to say, after that date I have chosen to speak to people on the phone first. Hope everyone is laughing!

Let me tell you some more and fill you in on what's happening in February already. Remember Sam who I mentioned, and we went on two dates to the same restaurant? Well, he was supposed to be in two weeks of training for a new position in sales. He was in one aspect of sales and decided to go into a different aspect. I understand we all need a change. He has many years of experience. He said he would call me on a certain night and didn't. Two nights go by, and I think he must be busy. I get it, stuff happens. He calls while I'm talking to a relative for quite a long time and I wasn't going to call him past a certain time. Then, he texts the next day I'll call tonight, doesn't call again in two days. We finally catch up over the weekend and he stopped going to the sales program after the third day. He was scheduled for five full days. The company did a "bait and switch" as he calls it. Unfortunately, things happen. I understand. We talk on Saturday about when we could possibly get together again, and I reply I'm busy, I made plans because I thought you would be in training for two weeks as originally scheduled.

I haven't seen girlfriends in many, many months and we are getting together for a happy hour that has been scheduled for weeks. That is scheduled for a Wednesday evening after work. On Mondays, I usually go to a non-denominational church service which is less conventional than my usual Catholic service, and I get a great deal of peace and spirituality out of it. On Thursday, during the same week, we're celebrating another girlfriend's birthday. I replied to him on the phone I'm available on Tuesday or Friday. I even offered to meet him closer to his side of town and named a few areas. I said you'll have to let me know the restaurants in that area because I'm not familiar with them. Let me take a step back. He suggested going to dinner at the same restaurant we'd already been to twice in a different part of town. I said, let's try somewhere different. I mean really, dinner there three times?

On Sunday, he knew I was driving up to New Jersey to visit my son at college. I don't normally visit, but it was a milestone birthday and I wanted to spend a lunch was my son and have an alcoholic beverage with him since he was turned 21. He calls me and I don't pick up as I'm driving. I was really concentrating. I listened to the voicemail, and he was replying to a voicemail that I left him the day prior which he never listened to. Makes me wonder about this guy? While I'm driving, I get a text are we on for Saturday? I did not respond because I'm driving, then went on to visit my son and his girlfriend. He hasn't called since; this is Tuesday evening we're supposed to meet. No word from him at all. My frustration is... the last thing we hung up with is Tuesday evening works well; let me know when and where you want me to meet you. What happened to Tuesday?

I know he's looking for another job. He's busy. It's like he fell off the radar. Here is another thing... During our conversation on Saturday, he was talking about looking for another job. He went on to say he really could retire, but he wants to keep working a bit. I asked him, how old are you? He replies, I'm 60, you know I don't look it and I don't act it. He proceeds to chuckle. I reply, oh really? Your profile states you were 56. He says, yes, that's a mistake; I can't change it.

Let me just say that I have dated older men, up to 11 years older in fact. That does not bother me. The fact that he didn't fess up about it until after two dates, texts, and talking on the phone, bothers me. The fact that the first date he's going on and on how much he loves his house and it's five miles from where he grew up. He doesn't ever see moving away. The third thing is... I'm thinking he's busy training Wednesday night and Thursday night. He is supposed to have homework after each day of class. He came home by Wednesday night.

Thursday, he's telling me via text how crazy of a day it's been and the same on Friday.

Now, ladies, things happen. Mistakes are made when inputting the age. He fat-fingered it. Again, my point is... We went out twice to dinner, talked on the phone quite a bit. It should have come up by now, hey, my age on the profile is incorrect.

Let me explain about his hands and how they were a dead giveaway. It's funny, at these two dinners, when I was looking at his hands, they weren't hard looking like a home contractor that works with his hands or a machinist. Quite the opposite... they looked super soft and almost elastic-like. You know what I mean? I know you can picture them yourself.

This guy friend, he said if his hands look like that, he was probably older than 60. Who knows at this point?

Lesson: Feel free to be inquisitive, Ladies and Gentlemen. If something seems a bit odd, call it out gently and respectfully.

Remember, when I mentioned the gentleman, Barry, who I met on a birthday through mutual friends? He contacted me once and we exchanged a few texts back and forth. I remembered his birthday about two weeks after the original contact. Here it is three weeks later and never heard another word. I feel like I'm the queen of getting ghosted. I say because the men of today like ghosting me. LOL!

I mentioned earlier that I had gone on the same dating site a year prior for a six-month duration. I think I met five guys; I ended up dating one gentleman, Sean, for three months. We talked for hours on the phone. We really got to know each other and talked about many things, including travel, retirement, children, divorce, etc. I'm not saying he was the one. I will say though there was definitely an emotional connection. When you talk for that many hours, it happens. There were at least four occasions where we talked for over two hours during a weeknight. We spoke at least five out of seven nights of the week. We were an hour apart, geographically speaking. Since we talked so much on the phone, we were building that connection. I even introduced him probably within a month to about five girlfriends. I don't usually do that! NEVER!!

They have to pass my own tests before I do that. LOL. I put him through my own regimented questioning and dating.

However, I felt there was a connection; I wanted my girlfriends to meet him, and I wanted us to have fun! My girlfriends seemed to like him, and he got along with anybody. He was also very generous, and he bought the group a round of drinks the first time he met them. He purchased a property in Florida that he intended to put it on rent on Airbnb for investment purposes. His mother and stepfather already lived in the area

One evening, out of the blue, he calls and tells me that he's picking up and moving to Florida. We will no longer date. I was utterly shocked!! This came out of the blue. We had talked about relationships, we both wanted one, he said he might go to Florida for a few months, and we would come back. We could handle that. He would be a "snowbird' and go back and forth. Needless to say, I was upset. Not so much crying, but I was angry and hurt. I thought all these hours on the phone just got flushed down the drain. We had dated for about three months. Time moved on, I dated a few others. The holidays came. About eight months after the breakup, around 10:30 at night, my phone rings. I don't pick it up because usually, when Sean and I spoke, we would be on the phone for over an hour. I just wanted to try to unwind and fall asleep. Then. I get a single-word text that states, 'Hey'. Again, I don't respond that night.

About midmorning, I reply to his text and state, 'Good morning, how are you doing?' Few hours go by no word. So later that evening after dinner, I text, 'Hope all is well!' I get a response. 'Are you ready for this one?' The response was I was feeling a little lonely and thought I would say hello. Once again, I must be Dear Abby. When you're lonely, just give me a call. Really? Is this what I've come to? 1-800-phone-a-friend!! No comment. I just can't even anymore. I just can't! We did not end on bad terms, or maybe we did? I was very angry in the end. So, it goes.

Lesson: In dating life, you cannot get hopeful, excited, and think there is a chance because it all comes tumbling down. Like I said, not sure I knew if he was the one, but the way it was handled and how abrupt it was takes one back.

CHAPTER 13

MEN'S DATING PROFILES

Where do I begin? Each night, I click on that discover button to see who is new. Can I just say I'm sick of seeing pictures of guys holding fish? Really, gentleman? Let me give you some tips to take pictures for dating apps, and believe me, I am no selfie queen!

First of all, for the first headshot that people are going to hit yes or no, as in skip or like, have a close up, a smile would help also! Don't take it from far away, don't stick your tongue out! That's kind of gross and weird at the same time.

Show your eyes! What do they say... Eyes are the window to the soul. Gentlemen, the ladies would like to see your eyes. That, with a smile, would make our day! Can I say something else here? Don't hold the phone down by your crotch or your belt. No, I am not looking! It's just an odd angle.

Nor do I want to see up your nose. Really, nose hair is not a turn-on. Now if you hold the phone above you to take a picture, I'd rather see a bald spot. That's all good. We're not youngsters anymore. You should have other pictures with it. I think three to five pictures to upload for your dating profile. Maybe I am mistaken? At least, three in total and one with a headshot. Minimally, one full-length picture which shows your height is valid. Another one could be a photo taken far away like hiking or finishing a marathon. This will show everyone you're engaged in some sort of activity, even if it's a beach scene or fishing.

As much as I don't think fishing tells much about a person, I should have the fishing scene down by now. I should know **all types of fish living off of the Chesapeake Bay with as many fish pictures as I've seen of guys holding up their prizes**! LOL!! I really get that men enjoy fishing. It's just that the women don't get the full physical facial view of the man. I mean we all have to have our own activities, most certainly. At this point, I know a striped bass from tuna from mackerel and salmon.

Now, let me tell you the pictures that don't get any attention. The pictures where men are sticking out their tongue. Really? How old are we? I know you men are trying to be funny and maybe it's just my opinion. We're all entitled to one! It really does nothing for me to see your tongue, I must say. The other pictures are, as cool as it is, of men wearing their sunglasses. Only have one picture wearing your sunglasses and upload it. Some of these men's profiles have four, five, and six pictures and they're wearing their sunglasses in each and every one. I mean I get it you're in your car, by your car, motorcycle, even the boat. I am one for protecting your eyes. You need to!! Then, there's overkill with pictures wearing your sunglasses.

Gentlemen, you know what else would work for you? If we see you in a casual outfit, as in a bathing suit at the beach, shorts, whatever. Another picture could be a more dressed-up outfit, such as jeans and a nice shirt with a jacket. Gosh forbid, a suit or a tuxedo would even make the lady more interested in that man. I understand the dressed-up look isn't for every man. Most certainly, not. My only point is to make yourself look presentable.

Oh, and here's another you should not do. Don't take pictures with your shirts off. Really? I know there are some women out there, probably a lot of women out there, who go for that look. Hey, I am not saying that wouldn't get a rise out of me myself! However, is it really needed with the rest of the photos? What happened to building an emotional connection? Sure, there has to be a physical attraction too!! Absolutely! I am just saying don't put these weird pictures on your dating app. I mean, I have seen guys post pictures of themselves in Halloween costumes. How about those pictures where you men pose in a bathroom? Are you a salesman for that tile company or what? Really?

I'm also a person who favors sunset pictures and palm trees along with any beach scene. Different places are great!! Yet can we not have every picture of the places you traveled to? We need to see the real human behind the picture. That stuff is just fluff. You are hiding behind the camera, literally.

Also, I'm a pet lover as much as anybody else. I love dogs. I prefer them over cats. Let's not have 10 pictures of your dog. Just saying. I know you like the aerial view, like on top of his head then from one side, then from the other, then him laying around, maybe doing a trick. We only need to see so many pictures of your pet. We love those companions, but really? These are just a few tips to think about.

Lesson: You don't need to hire a photographer, nor do you have to be a selfie expert. Just a few simple pictures are all that's needed.

CHAPTER 14

MID-FEBRUARY 2023

It's almost mid-February of 2023 and let me give you an update. I never heard from Sam. The last phone conversation, we agreed we were both able to get together on Tuesday or Friday. He replied I'd rather sooner than later. I said then Tuesday, it is. You let me know when and where. Never heard where, when, or anything else. Don't you think he should have texted, called or something, especially if he was that interested? I guess he is too busy looking for a new job? Who knows?

Never heard from Tom of the water town anymore whose son lives with him either. See, ladies, these men email you back and via the dating app. Then, ask for your phone number and you text back and forth. Very, very rarely is there a phone conversation. Third step, they finally suggest meeting. You meet, have a few dates and that's that. No one wants to put in any effort. They suggest moving away and retiring and you coming with them or staying where they are, and you meet up and date every now and then. WTH?

I met the fifth gentleman from Match. Let's call him Dan, who is an attorney, and lives about 45 minutes away. We had a few phone conversations. The time passed quickly on the phone. He is extremely intelligent, very well-versed; we talked about various subjects both on the phone and in person. He has only one child, a daughter about the same age as mine. He happens to be Jewish. I am Catholic. Now, before you say anything, I realize not a lot of women would date outside their religion. He is not the first Jewish gentleman I have met. I am not opposed to dating a Jewish gentleman. The other gentleman I dated, was not stuck in his religion at all. His wife, the mother of his children, was Catholic as well.

Anyway, Dan did look like his pictures which was quite refreshing! We decided to meet like a distance halfway for both of us. He suggested 3 p.m. and I said 3:30 p.m. will work better and explained about my night shift.

We're going to meet for a glass of wine, fine! I was on my way; he texts me that he had gone to the original place we were supposed to meet, and it was crowded and loud. He found another place. He was kind and considerate enough to text me where that was, that it was across the street, and sent the address. He got points for that. LOL!

Unfortunately, I arrive a few minutes late because I had to find parking few blocks away. The place we met was a Mexican place. We both have a Mexican beer, Modelo. We have good conversation. However, it was almost a monologue. This gentleman would do a lot of talking and he asked a ton of questions I might say. I can't say it was an interview, but it wasn't personable either. It was about where we grew up, food we like, areas around Maryland. He was from New England area. He asked me my favorite food, where I like to vacation, and travel to. It was fine, but he did a lot of talking. He told me to dress casual, which I did in jeans, booties, and a medium weight sweater. He was in jeans and casual shoes himself, along with a long sleeve golf-type shirt. However, he was super thin. So thin, almost like a toothpick. There was no muscle. Does he ever workout or only walk and hike?

Here's another thing. Though, he did look like his pictures, his hair was rather interesting, and I tried not to stare at it. It was salt and pepper, but mostly pepper. It wasn't gelled up and spiked that way. I could have accepted that, and he had a picture on his profile like that. It wasn't combed down either. It was somewhat in between. It was as if he never bothered to comb it! I couldn't help, but I tried not to stare at him. It was quite distracting! Like couldn't he comb his hair? Did he not look in the mirror before he walked out the door? It wasn't like it was rainy, it was a tad breezy. That would not have made his hair look like this! Truly, it was like he never combed it and in the back. I mean, you think you could just feel it and see. It was very odd.

I went to the bathroom after about an hour just because I had one beer and water, and water on the way to meet him. I went back to my seat. We did manage to get a plate of plain nacho chips with salsa. The bartender asked Dan if he wanted another beer, he responded no, I said the same. After an hour and a half, I said I better be heading back. I said that because he said he was going to his daughter's place in College Park where she attends. She and her roommates invited their parents' dinner. He had to pick up some wine on the way as well. That was at least an hour's drive. You never know what traffic you could hit, and he wanted to pick up wine along the way and was unfamiliar with where to.

He asked for the bill. Like I always do, I offered to split it or leave tip. He replied no, but thank you. He walked me to the door, and he's parked in one direction, and I am parked in another. He didn't offer to walk me to my car or watch me. This was fun, he stated, and that was it. It was rather odd. I have not heard from him, though it's only been 24 hours. Not a follow-up text like nice meeting you, no thank you, or I don't think we're a match, whatever it may be.

Remember I mentioned Barry, who I met on a birthday about a year and a half ago? Out of the blue, he texted me on Saturday and asked if I have any plans tonight. This was in the early afternoon. I said no, nothing in particular. That was my response I texted back. He didn't ask me out. About an hour and a half later I text, what are you up to? He stated he was available. That was it. I told him I was going to meet a girlfriend for a drink. I text him that while I was en route to meet gentleman number four. Talked to text, that is! Obviously, I didn't text him when I was with this other guy. Yet, when I went to the restroom, I sent him a quick text. He said he could meet, and do I want to meet? I replied I can I'm leaving my girlfriend shortly. After Dan and I parted ways, I got in my car, locked the doors as I always do. I looked at my phone as I turned on the engine and he said when do you want to meet? I said I'm leaving XYZ area now. I can meet you wherever. I didn't want to go past the general area, which was halfway for both of us all the way back to my home to let the dog out and come back.

As I pull out of my space and begin driving, he calls me. Imagine that! He tells me he is available now. I replied name your place and when. He suggests a Mexican restaurant on my way home and not far from his home or mine. Mexican must have been the theme that day. Meet for a drink at a Mexican restaurant and now, this one. Do you really want to know my thoughts on why Mexican? I am certain you can figure it out.

He asked me to check Google Maps as to how long it will say, and I said I will as soon as we get off the call. I put it in my phone, and it would take me about 15 minutes, and he said the same thing. I waited in the parking lot for him.

He called me and he was on his way. He said his directions said it would take him about seven minutes and I sat in my car in the parking lot. He met me at my car. Now, ladies, I know this was last minute and all very spontaneous. Let me just say... I stepped out of my comfort zone. Everything is usually planned with me. However, this time I thought, let's go for it!! He had been texting me, then stopped, and ghosted me. I seized the opportunity. I enjoy his company, he's not bad-looking at all! He owns his own business, and mechanical sense. We had gone on a few dates prior. Very few, I might say.

He greets me with a peck on the cheek, and we proceed into the restaurant. There are a bunch of people waiting. I explained I had to use the restroom really quick. We found two seats at the bar that way we didn't have to wait. He pulls out the barstool for me and we start talking. He begins teasing me all over again. Let me just set the tone and the background for you. I was still in my jeans, medium-weight sweater, and booties from the meet and greet for gentlemen number four. Barry shows up in shorts, tennis shoes, and a sweatshirt. Not that it was cold here. It was around 5o, but I knew once the sunset that it would get chilly, and darn if it didn't. I asked him if he was cold and he says no. My point is... He didn't take the time to get ready. This is how spontaneous this was. We were talking, catching up, he's been on various dating apps, and we were exchanging dating stories. We talked about his daughter, who is within a year of my daughter's age. We spoke of his divorce. We were talking to the people on either side of us. He really can be fun. We had a great meal, only one beer. I did offer to split the bill as well this time and leave tip. He took care of everything instead.

I told him how I was documenting my experience on the dating app and the people I meet. He proposed at that time that we both go into a business venture together. Stay tuned and we'll see if it ever happens?

Here's the kicker... I bet he gained 15 pounds since I've last seen him in a year and a half. Fifteen pounds is not a super big deal. Yet, he needs to lose it. The belly is a bit much. I work hard to keep my petite figure as it is. I may not have an upper chest cavity. I was never born with those!! I even deflated when I nursed both of my children. Nonetheless, I really work out from my butt to my hips, to my stomach, not to mention my arms and especially my legs. I was just very surprised at his weight gain. Though, I couldn't tell. Maybe it was because he had a big sweatshirt on? I will give him the benefit of the doubt.

He walked me to my car, gave me a peck on the cheek, and we were teasing one another. He tells me to stay in touch and I reply I will try to. When I texted him Happy Birthday, I didn't get a response. I reminded him of this. He replied, you received a response, just a few weeks later, saying what do you have going on? LOL. We both laughed. That meant his text from that afternoon earlier in the day. We were together for about an hour and a half. He was tired; he wanted to go home.

Here it is little after 7 p.m. on a Saturday night, we parted ways, and I'm home by 7:45 p.m., take care of the dog, let him out, and fed him. Barry let me know he was home, and I was composing my text to him saying the same thing when his text came through. We proceed to text for about two hours after that. Apparently he said he went home and showered, but something told me that he came as he was, after doing things around the house. He texts at 9:15 p.m. he was going to bed. Now, I'm the one who had a night shift, the night prior, came home, and only got four and a half hours of sleep. LOL! See, I have more energy than these men. Laughing yet?

Barry and I are less than six months apart in age. He is very mature and has his own business. He has an idea of what I do. I found this very interesting that while we were eating, he suggested about moving to Florida. If we sold both our houses, we could move down there together. I just looked at him. I said I wouldn't make what I make down in Florida because it's cheaper cost of living and salaries aren't the same. He replied, you wouldn't need to because you sold your house and you'd be with me. Isn't this all very interesting? I haven't heard from him in basically a year and a half, we text a little bit, he ghosted me again, and now this. I find this all quite amusing.

The next day, Sunday, he does stay in touch. He texts about midafternoon, stating it was a nasty day, which it was. We text during the Super bowl. Here's the thing... He isn't into football, which I am! I understand the whole took a knee thing which didn't sit well with many people. That was a few years ago. He doesn't watch the local news either which is certainly not the first guy I have dated that does that. I'm getting to know more and more people that do not watch the local news. I try to avoid it myself except for weather and sports. We were texting a bit and all of a sudden, he states at 8:35 p.m. on Sunday night of the Super Bowl that he's going to bed. Not sure if I ticked him off or said something that frustrated him or what? Again, I tend to be a night owl. I know he gets up early like 4:30 in the morning, he may do invoices and administrative work, then gets his day going. He may be depressed too? Who knows? He should be working out. Did I say that? More to follow.

As I mentioned, I am Catholic. I do try to make mass. I do not go every week and sometimes I miss two to three weeks in a row. I do try, however. As I missed yesterday evening, I decided to go to my local parish at 11:00 a.m. mass this Sunday morning. I run into a few people I haven't seen in a bit. Our children grew up together at the same elementary and middle schools, they took the same religious education class that particular night, etc. I tend to sit in the back of the church. I was a few minutes late. I am praying and meditating. I'm watching people come back from communion and going to their pew. I see this woman return to her pew and I'm thinking she looks familiar. I'm thinking, could that be *her?* Is that who I think it is? I've only seen her twice, I think? Maybe even once? However, when I met her, I kept thinking to myself I've met this woman before. I even said to my son I know her from somewhere and I thought it was the local Athletic Club where I belonged for many years. As we receive the final blessing, the recessional starts. She looked straight at me, smiles, and waves. It's my ex-husband's girlfriend!! Keep in mind he lives in the next county away about 45 minutes away. Only me Lord, only me! I go to church to pray and run into my ex-husband's girlfriend. That makes number 5 as in his fifth major relationship!!! Now, I figured out where I knew her from when I met her. Church!! Now, it's come to that I can't even go to church and feel safe or at peace. My one place of solitude. I run into my ex-husband's girlfriend. Only me!

CHAPTER 15

FEBRUARY 2023 IS FLYING BY

Well, I've been keeping myself busy in this month of February. I visited my son a few weeks ago. I'm scheduling meet and greets. Let's recap. Never heard back from Sam, two dates at the same establishment and that was it. Never heard back from the guy, Cameron, I met for a date locally here for dinner and the one that said I'll get this time if you get next time. I can't help I had plans for the following Saturday that I had scheduled for many weeks. The other guy, Rich, who's getting ready to move to Key West and lives on a boat. Never heard from him. Tom from the watertown went MIA as well. You see, ladies and gentlemen, it seems like we just e-mail back and forth, and you become pen pals. Then, somebody works up the courage to ask for phone numbers. We exchange phone numbers, text back and forth, and finally scheduled date to meet have a few dates and here we are. Never heard from Dan, the lawyer, either. Very odd. I'm just so done. I would say it's me and take this personally. Yeah, I have enough guy friends that are saying no it's not you, the women out there are nuts too.

Barry and I exchanged a few texts last week. He sent a Happy Valentine's Day emoji, he hurt his neck, and a few days later I asked how it was he said getting better slowly. That was it. He hasn't asked me out and here we are. The more I think about it I don't think we would be a good match. He's my same age basically five months older. He goes to bed by like 8:30 -9 p.m. Maybe he doesn't want to text anymore? Just say you are not going to text not texting anymore, but really? I tend to be a night owl and I still get up. I've been told I have a lot of energy. I know that for a fact that I do. Also, he does not watch the local news. Though I know a few people that don't. OK no problem with that. He also doesn't watch any football, he would rather do other stuff. OK I know people that do that too, But when the Baltimore Ravens make it to the playoffs, you got to watch some of the games or the Super Bowl. He wasn't watching any of that. Like there's more to life than staying in. I get it too, but you have to get to a point. And I'm not going over his house just to hang out, watch movies and Shazam (you know what I mean, I know you do). I know I am all that, but he has to work on losing that weight for his own health.

I had a great President's Day weekend in 2023! On Friday, I work my usual night shift, but I met my fifth gentleman from Match.com. I stepped out of my comfort zone. I actually had a date for the first time ever with a guy with the same first name as my ex-husband!! This is progress for me because I swore all men sharing his same name were awful. LOL! Let's call him Same Name #1 or SN#1 for short. He is the sixth gentleman I have met.

We have been emailing, then progressed to texting. He asked if I wanted to meet up and I said sure we could meet. He is six years older; he was taking friends of his down the beach for Super Bowl weekend. We finally decided to meet on Friday of President's Day weekend. We met at a local sports bar pub where they had live music around happy hour time. They have good food, it was crowded, and live music. Unfortunately, the music was quite loud for that time of the evening. We had a few beers and we talked for over two hours, almost three. He is a great conversationalist. He dressed nice even for a sports bar. He is very interesting; owns multiple businesses, he's in the food industry, he has rental properties. He really took care of his children and has been divorced for quite a long time as well. It was a nice evening out. We were talking about children, and he says his adult daughter lives not far from this local pizzeria sub shop, which has great crab cakes. I said, oh, I don't live far from there either and he named the road. His daughter, who has a son, and I happen to live on the same road!! Only me. It's all good.

Unfortunately, his father was taken to the ER right before we met. His parents are in a neighboring state, so he was leaving the next morning to go see them. He did text over the weekend and by Monday planned to meet for the following Friday. That's how it's done!! He did ask me out for Wednesday, but that Wednesday is Ash Wednesday and I will be going to mass directly from work. He understood. We shall see what happens by the second date.

I took off night shift for that Friday as the following day I'm leaving early to see my daughter in a neighboring state, but it's like a four-hour drive and I will need rest to drive about eight hours or more in two days. I miss my children so much. I never really thought being an empty nester would have been like this.

That was Friday evening, then on to nightshift. I came home did my usual routine of taking care of the dog, and I go to sleep. I slept later than usual. I was having terrible sinus trouble because our lovely weather has fluctuated so much this winter and it's mostly warm when it should be cold. So I caught up on some things.

I get ready to go to mass at 5:30 p.m. at my church, which is less than two miles away, and I come home to eat dinner and then go to a neighboring sister parish. They were having a denim diamonds fundraiser. The ticket was inexpensive enough, and I support all these fundraising causes, why not? Again, I stepped out of my comfort zone. I attended an event by myself where I would know no one. I am social, but it was awkward to walk in solo. I introduced myself to the gentleman at the front table who I emailed. I began talking to one of the men at the table and he too works at the same base as I. Actually, he works in the same building where I work nightshift. I would never see him though, as I'm not there during normal daytime hours. I went to a table and was sitting by myself. I had gotten a drink with the drink tickets I bought and put some tickets in the silent auction baskets. This woman came over and invited me to sit with her and her husband. I told her I didn't want to intrude, and I was almost tearing up that someone reached out to me because then I didn't have to sit alone. It was awkward. I bet there weren't 80 people at this event, but it was all for a good cause. I proceeded to talk to this lovely couple. They were filling me in on how many years they have been in the area, where they volunteer, where they live, their children. It was very interesting and I'm so glad I ventured out. Also, the deacon that just officiated at 5:30 mass I attended was there, so I went to the deacon and spoke to him.

We begin talking, he too works at the same military base as I, but in a different government building. We exchanged business cards. He told me to stop by if I'm ever in that building. He invited me to the Irish dance that parish is having in a few weeks. The gentleman at the front table did the same thing! I also exchanged business cards with one of the men at the front table. The deacons both said to me, "I am out of my robe and please feel free just to call him by his first name." I was really taken back, very different. It was refreshing! I have two networking contacts out of the event. I met different people; they all invited me back for a fish fry every Friday during Lent and they just don't serve fish. I will definitely go! Not sure I can attend the dance, which is ahead of the holiday when I think I have to work nightshift Saturday instead of Friday. The event was supposed to go from 7 to 11:00 p.m. It really emptied out by 9:30 p.m. I help stack chairs and clean up. I was home 10:15 p.m. All round, it was a delightful evening! I'm glad I pushed myself out of my comfort zone not once, but twice in two days! The people were lovely, it reminded me of my values and what life is truly about.

By the end of the weekend, I met the seventh gentleman from Match.com, Gabriel. We arranged to meet at a local Italian restaurant, he beat me to the place and then he texted me and said they're closed. We proceeded to meet at another restaurant across from that original location. I met him at the bar. He had been sick for a while, so we have been texting for a few weeks. We begin by talking about careers, he's an accountant for DOJ, start telling me about a few cases here and there. Now, let me interject right here and now... my former husband was in the accounting field. Those men can be rather dull!! Been there, done that.

I mentioned my career. We start talking particulars about jobs, places of employments, work locations, teleworking. We then move onto kids, or I shall say young adults. We discuss where they went to high school, where they go/went to college now, what is their field of choice. This was after talking about dogs, moving, Catholic churches. He mentions his daughter's name, when she went to high school, and I reply my daughter graduated that year from the same private Catholic high school. Our daughters graduated together. This is another reason why I don't like to date men in this local county; everybody knows everybody else. Dear Lord.

In the middle of the discussion about churches, he mentioned he attended the Catholic church I attend. I replied I recall you, your wife, and daughter. I stated I can picture your wife right now. Though, I forgot her name. I did ask how long they had been married. He replied 32 years and he's only been divorced two years, which meant he got divorced during COVID. He stated they just grew apart. Remember that because something just doesn't seem right....

He is close to six-foot, hair cut very short, kind of scholastic looking with his glasses. He mentioned he lost 20 pounds by not eating carbohydrates and not drinking beer. Yet, he can drink hard liquor and wine. While we were together for two and a half hours, he ordered an Old-fashioned, and two glasses of Chardonnay. I was just surprised he ordered a third drink when we were really done and wrapping up our evening.

Physically, he is not bad-looking, but he is not a head-turner either. LOL. He's intelligent, we spoke of many things. His sense of humor did not shine through. He didn't seem to laugh or smile about anything. We did not talk about travel. He took his kids to the same Ravens game I took my kids this past season. That game happened to be the coldest game on record. We spoke a lot about children, growing up in this area, where we both grew up with the Catholic education.

We did not speak of how long he has been on Match.com, how many dates he's had, his experiences. We spoke a lot about his dogs. He seems to walk them every night, and they are his pride and joy. He takes walks but doesn't exercise—lifting weights, tennis, or any cardio. The muscle mass is not there.

We each ordered two different kinds of salads. I must say the restaurant we ended up eating had a wonderful selection of food. I had a tall beer and he had three alcoholic beverages. I had enough of this salad with steak that I took a small amount home and had it for lunch the next day. The bill comes and as usual I offer to pay my portion. He says no, but you can get the tip. As usual, I only have $20s as the ATM only distributes $20.00 bills. He does ask for change from the bartender. The bartender gives me four $5 bills. The tip I leave it's just about the cost of my salad. With all the beverages and his salad, the bill added up. Now, why would you suggest that I tip especially on the first meet and greet? Ladies, how would you feel about that? I do offer. I could tell he has money working for the DOJ several years. His eldest child, a daughter has graduated from college and has been working on her own. His youngest, a son, is still attending college. At this time, my daughter is still completing her master's degree and only began working full-time about six months ago. My son is going on to law school as well. He knows I work two jobs, I told him that. I know this is a picky inny thing about the tip, but the whole notion just gets to me. He should be ready to date and pay after us texting for three weeks since he has been sick and it being our first date.

He did text me a little bit after our date. He also texted the next day and suggested we may meet for National Margarita Day. However, it happens to fall on Ash Wednesday and I'm going to a service right after work. That was that. Who knows? More to follow.

We are approaching the last week in February 2023. I have met my eighth gentleman from Match.com. He suggested a restaurant closer to him. I, on the other hand, replied I wasn't comfortable with that restaurant. Let me explain why... my ex-boyfriend, John, goes there. The other gentleman I dated, William, has been known to frequent there. Potentially, another gentleman I'm interested in, whom we've been friends with for years, goes there. Not only that, but it also has live music, which

I love! However, it is way too loud. Regardless, I recommended another place for us. He comes from one direction, and I come from the other. It worked out, he was there and already seated at a small table. I came out of my comfort zone again. This man is the second guy with the same first name as my former spouse. I'm doing this!! This gentleman, we will call him— the same name #2, or SN#2, is 59, a building engineer, and originally, from a different county. I mentioned that for a reason. Stay tuned.

The waiter takes our drink order. He ordered a Corona, and I order my usual, a Coors Light. That's my standby, especially when I'm driving. We talk and talk and talk and talk. He is not from the same county originally. Rather, he moved from an area where a bunch of my cousins live. He decided to move out this way and I was a little surprised. He has a Harley-Davidson motorcycle. He asked how I knew. I replied in one of the pictures, you were wearing a Harley-Davidson jacket, so I assumed. He just bought a 2023 super glide. OMG! He showed me a picture. Can you say a smooth ride?

He does not have any children and he is divorced. We didn't get into the semantics of that. We talked about various hobbies we each have, working out, traveling, the beach, riding motorcycles, blah blah blah. We finally ordered dinner. He orders the special of the day, which was prime rib. It was over $30 that came with two sides. I order a garden salad with grilled salmon. It was very good. I think he had an extra beer compared to me and he had a little bit of bourbon. He explained later that he loves bourbon with a steak, but he waited till after he ate to have it. We were there for quite a bit of time. There was a small band playing in the bar, which was on the other side, but we could still hear it. He kept the conversation going. He seemed interested in me. We were talking about houses and areas where we grew up, what he does, and where he travels for work. I was quite surprised I was there so long!! The time was passing, and we didn't order dinner for a bit. The dinner came out quickly and we were still talking. I was ready to go at about two and a half hours in. The waiter left the bill, and you could tell he was getting antsy as he continued to check on us. The gentleman goes to pay it and I did offer. He said no, so that was it. That bill had to be something with our meals, including the drinks, tax, and tip. We all know that everything has gone up since COVID.

We were wrapping up talking. Let me give you a little bit of background. This gentleman and I only exchanged two or three messages via the app. He never asked me for my phone number, my last name, or any other real details. It was one or two messages, and he said do you want to meet? I would prefer that. I was taken aback, but it was a public place, I told a few girlfriends about the time and place where I was meeting him. ALWAYS, ALWAYS do that, ladies!

He pays the bill, we're walking out. I happen to park next to his truck and didn't even know it. He asked me for my number, which I give to him because it's much easier to text or call someone than to keep going in through the app.

It was good until that point. Can I just say that, ladies? It really was. I haven't had a meet and greet last three hours in forever. I think that was a first! Never ever, ever has that happened. Usually, you meet for coffee or happy hour or drinks or ice cream or a walk even! Never a dinner like that!

If you're a gentleman reading this, take note. He went to kiss me goodbye and give me a hug. It wasn't a peck on the cheek; it was on the lips. Okay fine. He attempts to make out with me, standing up in the parking lot. I wasn't having it. I pulled away, gave him a hug, and said thank you. It was a really great date to that point!! There were people getting in their cars around us. It wasn't the time or place. I guess he was really attracted to me? Idk? We left it like that. I did get a text from him the next day. He texted me to call him when I got back in town as I was going out of town to visit my daughter for the weekend. He was a great guy, but I am not standing around a parking lot making out like we are 16, especially when there are about 10 people standing around in all directions.

I was supposed to have a second encounter with the SN #1. the one that I met about a week ago. He had some family matters come up with his older parents last weekend when his father was hospitalized. His father got discharged, and he came home after spending more time up there than originally anticipated. He has to return there again this weekend, which is a three-hour drive away so we both decided to cancel the date.

When I returned from visiting my daughter on the following night, I texted SN #2. I reached out to ask how he was doing; did he have a nice weekend? He replied, and asked how my weekend was, and mentioned we should get together again. I told him I was going to a concert on Wednesday that had been postponed for 10 months since band members got COVID. On Thursday, I'm meeting up with two girlfriends I used to work with and the last time we got together was eight months ago. I told him I could get together on Friday, Sunday, or next week. He replies let's just get together next week. I said OK. It seemed like he wanted to get together on Thursday, however.

Now, ladies, what do you do? I'm an empty nester now, I made it through COVID, and I am ready to do things. Sitting in this house all by myself, feels like it's a mansion and it's certainly not! When I say that, I mean it's me and the dog, and he snores just like a man. LOL. My only point is I make plans and do things. I'm catching up with people. That was that. He said he would stay in touch.

CHAPTER 16

MY GODMOTHER'S 90TH
BIRTHDAY CELEBRATION

On Sunday of President's Day weekend, 2023, was my aunt/godmother's 90th birthday party. I would not miss it for the world!! About six weeks prior, my aunt had a health scare. Her five children were in the midst of planning her party and everything was put on hold. My aunt, being the trooper that she is, made a full recovery and said go on with the party. We did just that!! Can you tell we are Irish Catholics? LOL.

It took place on a Sunday afternoon with all of her children, grandchildren, nieces and nephews in attendance. The food was delicious, the cake was yummy, the company was unbelievable! All of us Irish Catholic cousins gathered for the matriarch of the family. It was an event! My aunt happens to share the same birthday with a second cousin of mine who was also my junior groomsman at my wedding. He also has cerebral palsy. Rowan was so excited to share the day with her! My aunt is wonderful. I cannot say enough positive things about her. She has been such a role model in my life. The one thing my parents did do right was make sure that I had two wonderful godparents. Unfortunately, my godfather/uncle on my mother's side of the family passed away.

My godmother has been my strength, my role model, and my friend. She has been such an encouraging influence in my life and throughout, she always reminded me to have my faith in God and do what's right with integrity. She may be in her rolling walker that has a seat with it, but her mind is sharp as a tack, as they say! She does not miss a beat!! I had her laughing, was filling her in on my young adult children, and my life. Nothing like a good chuckle!! We both have fine hair; we laugh and joke about it. My aunt is my inspiration. I can't quite describe it. She and her sister, another aunt, each had five children. My godmother had a child and 18 months later had identical twins and went on to have two other children. Her sister had a set of fraternal twins and 18 months later had a child, and then two other children. They would banter about which was harder to have: an 18-month-old, then twins or twins, or 18-month-old twins, then a newborn? Ponder on that for a moment.

It was something to see when the sisters got close together and talked. It was lovely! They were holding each other's hands while they were talking. You saw the bond in the other's eyes and the camaraderie.

I caught up with all my cousins and their children, as well as their offsprings, who are now having kids of their own. The babies weren't there; only two came late in the day. Cousins I hadn't seen in years attended. My second cousins I babysat and now they're having children of their own.

We are also blessed. Everyone is healthy, good good-looking, gorgeous eyes with beautiful cheeks. The facial structure of both the men and women and how no one has aged!! Of course, there could be gray hair, but truly in the face, no wrinkles, no lines! We all made it through COVID, and they all have partners. I spoke to some of my cousins, and they were having a hard time even though they had each other. Imagine me who was solo?? When the kids left, what was I to do? COVID hit everyone differently, whether you had a partner or not.

I had an extraordinary day. I got home and it was surreal. I cannot put into words how it made me feel. I was taking it all in... the smiles, the hugs, the laughter the look on people's faces. They were asking me how my children were. I'm coming up on 20 years of being divorced, a.k.a. alone and raising the kids. I received many kudos and that's not my intention at all. Whereas they had both partners, it was solely me raising the kids primarily. It was even funnier, when I told people my ex-husband is on his fourth marriage and that it did not end well. LOL!

This was a day like no other and one that I shall always cherish. The stories that were told were some I hadn't heard before, and me in my fifties, that is odd. I laughed; I was in awe. I heard stories of the two sets of cousins growing up. My aunt, who had five boys, they always made everyone laugh. Everyone was laughing till we cried. It was too much fun!!

I heard another story about the aunt with five boys, how long she knew her now deceased husband before he proposed and the timeline of the dating to proposal to marriage. Something I never knew!

It was such an uplifting weekend. I did two things that made me step out of my comfort zone. I met wonderful people at the church event as well.

CHAPTER 17

MARCH 2023

As we concluded February 2023, I have met eight gentlemen from Match.com. This is certainly an improvement over the prior year. I had only met five men in six months of 2022. In the first two months of 2023, I have met eight gentlemen. Now, I will admit that I have not heard from the first five. You see how this plays out, ladies. Three of these gentlemen have been one-and-dones. What can I say? You see how this plays out? What is one to do?

I did have some interesting correspondence back and forth with a few gentlemen. Then either they don't ask you for your phone number and it ends. The other way goes that they do ask you for your phone number and they text back and forth and that's it. I'm finding men are interested, but they also still have their children. I'm a complete empty nester! I stay busy because I am an empty nester. I work two jobs, but I can also go meet people and do things.

Let me tell you one experience I had in the month of February that I'm trying to forget. A gentleman younger than me by about 11 years started messaging me and I replied to the emails. I did say to him, you do realize how much older I am than you? He replies, yes, but it doesn't matter to me. I thought interesting. Maybe he just wants a cougar? Could that be possible? Many people say I don't look my age. Keep in mind that he has a picture post of him in a uniform. He is in law enforcement in a neighboring county about 45 minutes away.

We begin to text. About the third text in, I get a text message that says would you be interested in being a Dom? Before I go ballistic, I had to Google to confirm what I thought. he meant. Sure enough, it was what I thought!! I reply to this gentleman, and I said that's not for me, please delete my number and I will do the same. I proceeded to do just that. See, you get all kinds. Truly, you do!

In January and February 2023, I kept busy. Obviously, with my full-time and part-time jobs, meeting these gentlemen, and of course, taking care of a home. That's not including taking care of the dog, and I happened to visit both of my children in two different states. What will March bring? We shall find out. Let's bring it on.

In the first week of March, I had two more dates with two different gentlemen. I should say one meet and greet and one date. You are wondering about the difference? The meet and greet is just that. You meet a gentleman for the first time, complete the introductions, and see where it goes. You can meet for coffee, drinks, ice cream. I've had many meet and greets. Even had one that just wanted to walk a local trail. Don't get me started on the epitome of cheapness! LOL!

Sometimes, you have a wonderful gentleman who even wants to take you to dinner. Don't get me wrong. I always offer to split the bill, though, the rule books tell you not to do that! After much reading, I'm being told I shouldn't even offer to pay and split the bill or tip. I mean, is chivalry dead or what? Now, a date is after the initial meet and greet, which is really just an introduction, as I said. The first date is the true date where more effort is put forth by the man, he suggests the place, the time that is mutual, and usually, he pays for everything including the tip! Just saying. That may not be true, and I realize some men, and women, may have a difference of opinion on this. That's fine. This is just one opinion. That is all.

Lesson: Ladies, if the man offers to pay for whatever event, including the tip, let him. It's really ok. I have a few girlfriends who have trouble allowing this.

Gentlemen, be real gentlemen and pay for it all, especially if you are very much interested in this lady.

On the first Friday in March, I had a meet and greet with my ninth gentleman from Match.com. He suggested a local Italian place very close to me which is fine. I love the place, good food, great wine. We arranged to meet, and unfortunately, the place was packed. No tables in the bar area or at the bar. This was a cold, miserable, rain blowing in your face Friday night. If I had not had plans, I would not have been out! We managed to go across the parking lot to another place, which is a seafood restaurant, to talk and have a few drinks at the bar. I was going to have the wine I love from the Italian place I'd like, but since we changed venues, I stuck with my Coors Light.

This gentleman named Matt is a widower; he lives about 15 minutes away; he has a son the same age as my daughter, and another son who's a junior in high school. He has been a widower for about 11 years. I didn't ask anything about that situation. We talked about where we grew up, where we went to schools, he is a project manager for a local defense company. I told him I'm a DoD contractor myself. I did not elaborate much. However, we both used to program in various software computer languages. I guess we have more in common than I thought because basically we're both geeks!! LOL Laughing yet? Takes one to know one, as they say.

He's tall, but not that tall, and he's extremely skinny. I feel when people are extremely skinny, it makes them look taller. Like there's no need meat on his bones. He's not a bad-looking guy, conversation went well, I do not know about his sense of humor. We were together for about two hours and 45 minutes. I was ready to go home as I was quite tired after my work week. He's very much a gentleman as he helped me take off my coat and put it back on again. He walked me to my car, gave me a hug, and a peck on the cheek. He texted me when he arrived back at his home and made sure I was home safe as well. He followed up the next day by sending me a few texts. This whole scenario is quite refreshing! Truly, it is!!

The dear Lord must have heard the thoughts in my head. This is way too coincidental. On Saturday afternoon, one of his texts was a picture of his gym equipment at his home. He says time for a workout now. I reply OK cool. Sooooo, he does workout which is great. He's just super skinny, there's no meat on his bones. He texts me again on Sunday to see if I would be interested in going out again. Now, I'm going to take this slow because I'm busy and already have plans. We shall see.

On Saturday morning, I had a date scheduled for brunch with Gabriel. He suggested this place about a half hour away that used to be happening place many, many years ago when I was underage. LOL. Now, it is a German restaurant, and I had heard many good things about it. We met at 10:30 a.m. for brunch. It's a sports bar with fabulous service, delicious food and a huge variety of drinks. It was $6.00 for a 32-ounce crush. Just saying. There were multiple menus. One for brunch and lunch and another for entrees like dinner. Then there was a third menu for the list of crushes, draft beers, German, Mexican beers, etc. You name it, everything!!

We spoke of a variety of topics, caught up on each other's children, different trips they were taking, and the trip I took to see my daughter. We spoke of friends he stays in touch with from high school and college, and an upcoming weekend trip he is taking. We mentioned different foods, raising children of all ages as they grow older. Here is another one, he told me prior that he lost 20 pounds basically being on the keto diet, where he cut out carbs and watched his sugars. However, he still does drink substantially. He walks his dogs for exercise and plays golf. He really does not do any cardio, lift weights, etc.

I'm telling you all of this, ladies, for a reason. At the time of writing this book, I am 53 and I am working two jobs. My full-time job is a DoD contractor, and a night shift job, part-time, usually Friday nights. I have a lot of energy and I don't mean hyperenergy. I'm just saying I can still get up, go to work, maintain a home, take care of the dog, while working two jobs. I need to find a man that has some decent energy! Now, I know two people need to have hobbies in common, shared interests, and shared values, most importantly. Really, I don't need somebody that goes to bed at 9:00 p.m. That is what I'm finding. Again, we shall see. The bigger concern or hesitation shall I say is... am I attracted to these men in any way to have an intimate relationship? They are not bad-looking per se, nothing that makes me feel comfortable or want to be naked with this guy. Let's just say that!!!

Please understand... I'm not one to get intimate quickly. Yet, I am no prude. However, with meeting nine of these gentlemen, no one is floating my boat in that way! I find a wonderful sense of humor very attractive, and it wants me to be closer to the gentleman. Right now, with the nine men that I have met, no one is doing a thing for me. I mean, not even a good make-out session, just saying!

So, it goes! I mentioned this to two girlfriends who happened to call me on this day and told this story. I said something must be wrong with me? They both said why? Two separate conversations and they said if it's not there, it's not there. Keep trying!! That's what I'm here to tell you to do... keep trying. Ladies and gentlemen, if you are not feeling something for the individual, you can't make it up. You cannot produce what isn't there in the feeling department. Does this mean you should get butterflies each and every time? No. You can try. Am I saying give it longer than two dates? That's up to you.

Maybe it's the romantic in me? Maybe it's the little girl in me who still believes in happily ever after somewhere? I attended a concert earlier this week. Many of Journey's songs are quite romantic. From Open Arms to Highway Run to Hugging. Touching, Squeezing Another (sing it with me, I can hear you!) It all brings to mind how humans were made for each other. As humans on this earth, we are not meant to be alone.

It's not even mid-March and the dates are picking up with some regularity. Imagine that! On Thursday, I had a date with SN #2. This gentleman does not text much during the week or stay in touch. Hadn't heard from him for almost a week and then on Monday he texts, hey how was your week and weekend? He asked how was this concert I attended. While we are texting back and forth, he asked, would you like to get together on Thursday? I said, sure. It was wonderful!!! He suggested a very nice place to dine and the time as well. See, how easy that can be, Gentlemen! Boom, done. It was great! No BS, nothing back and forth. We had a plan and four days' notice.

We met at 7:00 p.m. at the fine dining location. He is really a nice-looking gentleman, it's a shame he's the same name as my ex-husband. LOL. We sit there and talk a bit, and have an alcoholic beverage. Then, we order, and I got the salad with ahi tuna on it, which was delicious! He ordered the fish special of the day—the grouper. We were trying to be very healthy. Both of our entrees were delicious, served quickly, and our waitress was quite friendly. We proceeded to have another beverage and talked. We do have some things in common and the conversation flowed easily. He is always dressed nice, comfortable, yet stylish. He is nice looking. We talked about growing up in Maryland, this dating app, my kids, and he didn't have any children. He paid for the bill, though, I did offer. However, we ended up being the last couple in there on a Thursday night. Restaurants and bars aren't open as late as they were prior to COVID. I mean, this is a Thursday night. Really pre-weekend and this lovely restaurant and bar closed at 10:00 p.m. We felt bad we were the last ones in there.

He walked me to my car, gave me a hug and a kiss goodbye, and told me to stay in touch. Also, I did find out why he prefers to go out on Thursdays. He explained since he has moved to Harford County, the restaurants and bars are packed on the weekends. He prefers to avoid that, he enjoys going out during the week, and it's more relaxed. Well explained, I really do understand. It was a really lovely evening! This guy may have potential! Did I just say that? Especially with him being the same name, LOL! We shall see.

On Friday, very next day, I had a date with SN #1. Now, this gentleman is 59, only one year older than SN #2. He really doesn't exercise, except for taking his two dogs for a walk daily. I try not to compare these men when you build your funnel, as they say. Yet, how can you not? It's not really a comparison, it's more evaluating what you have in common, from values, morals, to hobbies to travel, and everything in between.

I met SN #1 at a bar/restaurant about 20 minutes away on a rainy, cold Friday night. I offered to meet him a tad closer to his home. He did offer to come to the county where I lived. I figured I saved a few minutes and miles. He arrived before I did as I had further to travel in rush hour traffic on a Friday night in the rain. We were seated at a table immediately. I ordered a beer as he already had one. Note: when I met both gentlemen and they arrived prior to me, they both had ordered a beverage. I find that interesting, not sure why? I guess you shouldn't keep a man waiting because they drink? Or they are nervous? Or really want to be courteous to the staff?

The waitress came by a few times, much like the previous night, and we were not ready to order. In fact, we hadn't even looked at the menu! Finally, we are ready. SN #1 stated he hadn't eaten all day. I do not know how people can do that. Myself, I eat all the time. Not good, I know. I also work out a little aggressively though. He also mentioned that he drove 250 miles that day for his job. I was glad I offered to meet him closer to his home. I ordered the mahi mahi tacos that came with long grain rice as it was a Friday in Lent and definitely something different to eat! He ordered the meatloaf that came with mashed potatoes and broccoli. The meal came quickly, the food was good, and the company was fine as well. We spoke about a variety of topics again. Mostly, it was about children, the adult children, a little about divorce, his parents, hobbies, etc. I did find out that on Thursdays, he bowls 10 pins. He went back to this sport after many years and enjoyed it. He went on to say that Fridays are his guy nights out and he likes dive bars. Ok, that is his things, nothing wrong with that. I took him away from the guys. Oh, well. I am much better company. LOL! Always!!!

This gentleman kind of acts older, but he is a good conversationalist. The conversation was easy. He explained the stages of the relationships as your children become more independent. I needed some reassurance with my parenting, more than anything else. We spoke of me going to the shooting range when my son took me. He was very knowledgeable about guns and his adult daughter wanted to learn to shoot. He offered to take me to the gun range as well, even has a contact of someone who teaches gun safety classes for women. He told me we will stay in touch and offered to take to me the gun range as the next date. We shall see.

On Saturday, I had my third date in a row. This date was with Gabriel, the one I met for dinner prior and brunch the previous week. He lives in the same county as me, so we decided to meet at a local Irish pub at 7:30 p.m. A few hours before our date, he texted me to ask can we could meet earlier because his plans to visit a friend recuperating from surgery fell through. I replied that was fine. I was going to go to 5:30 p.m. mass. He then suggested a different place for dinner. This place is rather new, tends to be packed especially on Saturday evenings, and a tad dressier. All these things I do not mind. The kicker is I was going to change my outfit. So, I said maybe you should call ahead? He did do just that; they only had a table available underneath the tent. Well, I'm in the northeast. It's still winter around the Chesapeake Bay and this particular weekend, it was quite windy! I decided to go with my less dressy outfit and I'm certainly glad I did! Because we were back at the Irish pub. I met him at 6:30, he did have a table. I'm glad I wore a heavy sweater because the door kept opening and it was rather chilly.

He already ordered himself a glass of wine, all three times I have met him he arrived before me, and he has already had a drink in hand of some sort. I thought after our first meet and greet about how much he had consumed in a short period of time. Was it a yellow flag or maybe I'm being a little paranoid?

The waitress came by a few times until we decided what we wanted. He and I are both Polish and he suggested this place because they serve stuffed cabbage a.k.a. galumki. Then, he told me he couldn't decide between three items, so he changed his mind again and I did as well. He ordered the stuffed cabbage; I ordered the Irish Stew with lamb and potatoes. It was excellent!! It was great on a cold evening. I also ordered a beer and he had himself another half a glass of white wine very quickly. The meal comes and he orders another beer as do I. I knew we would be sitting there talking a bit. Again, the conversation flowed very easily. We spoke about jobs, COVID, kids, the weather, and the upcoming St. Patrick's Day. He ran into a family he knew from the area. I hit the restroom and ran into a girlfriend's daughter and her husband and we spoke. I also told that young couple to come say hi to get their opinion of him and see what they pick up on.

Something just told me to do that. Intuition indeed?

After dinner, he proceeds to order an Old-fashioned, the drink that is. He did that on our first time out as well. They bring it and I can tell the color isn't quite right. I knew this because I used to bartend! He asks me to take a sip, which I did and it was sickeningly sweet. I told him they have to do something to it. So, he tells the waitress, she takes it back to the bar, and brings it back and it's a different color. Now, it's much darker and I can tell... it's much stronger. He takes a sip and says that'll put hair on your chest. He asks me to try it, so I took a tiny sip. It was extremely strong. He continues to take a few sips, the waitress came by again, and he said I need some water with this. She goes back to the bar again, they added water, and she gives it to him.

In the meantime, we discussed all kinds of things. I forgot that on our second date he asked me to opening day baseball here in this town, but he didn't tell me the actual day, so I never looked into it. He reminded me again. I replied I will investigate it and see if I can take the afternoon off. He was also talking about going to a hockey game. Also, he mentioned about playing golf together. I said I'm terrible. I haven't played golf in years. I would start at the driving range, then move on to playing 9 holes. He says oh no, oh no we must play 18 or it's nothing. I could see where this was going, his way or no way. He's sipping this drink, and he asked if I wanted anything else. I said I'll take an Irish coffee because he had this cocktail drink that was rather strong. I'm nursing the coffee and we're talking and talking and talking. In the meantime, the young couple comes over, I introduce them to him. He's talking to them. They say they're going across the street to another restaurant bar where there's a local band. He suggests we should go as well. Meanwhile, I'm tired, and it happens to be the night when we fast forward the clocks and lose an hour of sleep. Quite frankly, I was ready to go. He says come on let's just go for one. Did I mention that while he paid for the dinner, he asked me for tip of $20.00? My Irish Stew and two beers were close to that. My point is... I could have gone out to dinner with the girls or by myself spent that money on myself and the only thing different was the conversations. Really? It wasn't that great!! Just saying.

We go across the street to the other local restaurant/bar to hear the live music. It was a good band known around the area! I was done now though, very tired. I was ready to go home. We run into people I know, and I introduced him. I even knew one of the guys in the band who I haven't seen for many years pre-COVID. He orders a glass of wine and I asked for a beer. We continue to talk, listen to the band, having a good time except I'm really tired now. A little frustrated that he wanted to keep going. I looked at him and asked, aren't you tired? I might also mention that I asked his age while we were having dinner and I threw out a number when I should have had him tell me the number. The last time we were together I asked about his age also. He stated much about his divorce. I just found it odd that he was married 32 years and that they grew apart. Just saying. Don't just say that. It has to be something else.

I guess he was having more fun than I was. He leans over and asks, can I kiss you? I nodded; I didn't think he would do it there at the bar where it was crowded. I'm not a big PDA person, especially at the beginning of dating someone. Remember this is our third date, or really second, because the first time was the meet and greet. He leans over and goes to kiss me and I kind of gave him my cheek because we are in public. He says that wasn't any kiss and I laugh and shook my head.

He finishes that glass of wine and gets another, and I have maybe a quarter of a beer left. He asks, would you like another, and I said I've been done. I wait till he finishes about half of his class of wine, then tell him, I'm really tired and ready to go. He could have stayed, and I told him that. I was hoping to walk out by myself. He had way, way too much to drink. We walk out and we go toward his car as it was on the way to mine. He could have walked toward mine or even just watched me to my car. He gave me a hug and a kiss. I get in my car and drive home. Thank goodness. I was tired, done with drinking, done with him for the evening. Now, I know what you are thinking... if she were into this guy, none of this would have bothered her. You are probably right!

We both stated we would text the other when we got home. He texts me, "Great time tonight. But I think this has run its course. Take care of yourself and be safe. I'm sorry." Can I just say WTF? Really? You asked me to opening day for baseball, asked about going golfing, about going to a hockey game. Are you serious? I reply, yes, it was a great night indeed. Thanks so much.

OK I don't understand. Whatever. There you have it! Dating in your 50s with these messed up men. Just saying.

CHAPTER 18

MID-MARCH 2023

Where did the time go? We are into mid-March now. Last weekend was a busy weekend and filled with dates and this weekend, nothing. What can I say? It is also Saint Patrick's Day weekend. Saint Patrick's Day falls on a Friday this year and you know everyone's going to be out drinking.

This dating has been anything, but dull. LOL. Let me fill you in. Do you recall Gabriel who I had that last date with? It was our third date, and he texted me when he got home and said this has run its course after stating great night tonight? I hear from him the following Tuesday and get this long three-inch text stating that he's been hurt. Hey sorry. I understand love gets to you; I do! Let me tell you. Anyone that's gone through a divorce, has no desire to get HURT EVER AGAIN! The following all adds to it—different interpretations, and meaning of relationships, their version of the meaning of commitment. You would think it would be relatively simple terms. They are not!

I replied to this long text saying, "I understand, maybe you need to take a little bit of time for yourself, regroup. Whatever you need to do." I tried to be a friend, and understanding which I truly am, and go from there. That was it. On Wednesday, he texts me during the day while I'm at work and I'm busy, and I don't reply. I want this guy to figure out what he wants. I must admit I really wasn't that interested. The whole thing just ticked me off. But maybe it's me? On Thursday during the day, he texts me again, while I'm at work. I do not respond as I am busy! Thursday late afternoon, he texted me again I replied to that. Then, I get multiple texts on Thursday night. All I want to do is sit and chill. Now, I know he doesn't know this. I did tell him I had a big government meeting on Friday, he even asked how the preparation was going. He had some sort of clue. He continues to text back and forth on Thursday and asks what I was doing that weekend. He said he wouldn't mind grabbing a Guinness with me. I didn't want to tell him I don't drink Guinness. LOL! I repeated that he should figure it out himself because of what he told me on Saturday night when we got home. He replies just tell me if you want a casual or serious relationship. I didn't reply to that. I repeated you have to regroup.

Keep in mind, ladies, this is the third date. We're not talking marriage, commitment, or even exclusivity. He says, can't you give me an answer? I reply I know what I want. He writes to me, "I dodged a bullet," meaning me. I replied, that's funny. He says, have you ever thought that's why you're still single after 20 years? You have all this resentment toward your ex-husband. I'm going to tell you that was a low blow, and I could put on a few choice words here, but I will not. Definitely not a high-value man!!! I respond in 20 years, I've raised two kids, got my master's degree and my PMP certification. I have been in relationships, and one was even with an alcoholic, which I'll never do again. Of course, I did not know that. As soon as I figured that out, we broke up. When I wrote that back to him, I did not get a response. I did mention I thought he had a drinking problem. I told another girlfriend this story, she says it sounds like YOU dodged the bullet. Another girlfriend said he sounds unstable, like another project you would have to fix. Three dates and these guys go off?? That's two of my girlfriends' opinions.

Here's another thing. The gentleman that I mentioned and that I went out with the first one from Match called Tom from that water town. He sends me a message over the app, it says I hope you're doing well. I really enjoyed the time we spent together. First of all, how could you not? LOL!! Just kidding. I'm really not like that. Truly, two dates, two hours each and you had to run home to your 18-year-old son who lives with you? Don't forget that I didn't kiss him right outside in public when it was cold. OMG. He just expects more. I don't get it.

CHAPTER 19

END OF MARCH 2023

Well, mid-March rolled right into the end of March. Wonder how I'm doing on the dating? Here are the stats... I have met and gone out with nine gentlemen. Now, I can hear some of you saying, "Wow, that's a lot!" OR "How come she hasn't had more dates? What is she doing? Using these men? Is she a ho? What is she doing?"

Let me tell you, it's not like that at all. I've met these guys mostly for dinner, sometimes drinks, a brunch. Then, you don't hear from them. I don't get it. They're really busy with work and everything else. Quite frankly, they shouldn't be dating. Another guy says well, you can text me, so I text him a few times. It's nothing more than hi, how are you type of conversation about the week and nothing else. UGH!! Grrrrr.

I get to thinking... is it me?? Do I act interested? Do I give off the wrong signals? However, it's not just me. I belong to a group on Facebook where women write about relationship problems and it's like a blog. There are relationship coaches as well. Other women are writing in from all over the world, not just the United States, that they are encountering men who ghost them as well! It's not just me and I don't know if it's the circumstances? The times? Things that happen after COVID? Life, in general? But, why say I had a great time, I'll stay in touch, let's get together again and never even text or call? No one makes plans. The world is afraid to commit. I don't mean commit to a major relationship! I mean to commit to the next date, to get to know one another. I understand we all get busy with our lives. At this point in our lives, we're still concentrating on our careers and have responsibilities. We may be caregivers to elderly relatives; we also may make plans with friends and really be discovering life. I truly get all that!! Gentlemen, just don't say you're going to do something and don't follow up. We're not asking a lot here.

Lesson: Gentlemen, don't say you will be in touch if you are not feeling it. Just don't!! It's ghosting at its finest.

CHAPTER 20

INCIDENTS

Let me fill you in on some things to bring you up to date. First incident—do you remember I spoke of one of the first guys in this book, Jamie? He promised me many things that never came to fruition. It's a little past the middle of the month, just a few days passed his birthday. On a Sunday night, while finishing up watching Dateline, I receive a text out of the blue that says am I still blocked? Now, if I replied, he would know that he is not! LOL! I find out about a week after this message is received that his girlfriend, who happens to have the same name as myself, threw him a surprise birthday party. If she only knew that he had contacted me? What would happen? My point is... If he is in a relationship, why is he contacting me? If the relationship is all that, why is he contacting me? More than one girlfriend said he must be thinking about you! Who knows? No comment.

Lesson: Gentlemen, when a relationship is over, let it be in the past. Don't text the ex when you are with someone else.

Second incident—remember the gentleman mentioned earlier in the book named William? That relationship was extremely short-lived, but it was a relationship that never should have started. He had control issues; I couldn't go to networking happy hours. He was whiny, wanted things his way. In the end, it got back to me that he was quite disrespectful. I saw him through major heart surgery, I told him to go to the doctor and he would have died had he not gone. Then, he's talking about me very discourteously and disrespectfully.

On a Thursday night, while I'm sitting here watching my Law and Order TV shows in a row, I receive a simple text from him... thought of you. Again, I do not reply. If I do, he will know that he was unblocked. I never want to hear from him again!! I helped him recover, sat with him for hours upon hours, made him meals, cleaned his house. No freaking way! The very next day, while working my part time night shift job, I pick up the landline phone because sometimes people are in other buildings, and they report in. When I pick up the phone and answer, I don't say my name. The deep, gruffy voice on the other end says hey, what are you doing? I said who is this? You know who it is, was the response. He asks why do you hate me so much? He begins to tell me all the reasons that it is my fault. He states he was recovering; I didn't give him enough time to recover; he was busy with the business. He truly has no clue why, I told him multiple times why, about how things got back to me, and he was terribly disrespectful. At that point, another call came in on the landline. I told him I had to pick that up, he says call me back. There is no freaking way I would ever call him back. None at all!

Let's review this for a minute, shall we? Two of the gentlemen that I dated still contacted me. Now, why is that? Maybe they realized what they had? Maybe they realize I'm the next best thing? Just saying! Who knows? Truly, I do not. But why? That's the golden question! Why, ladies and gentlemen, does it take anyone in a relationship to realize what they lost when it's too late?!

Lesson for everyone: be respectful always, never take each other for granted. Keep things private and don't run your mouth.

Third incident—remember I mentioned DH? Well, I happened to find out from one of my children that he sent a group text to them was a picture of a house with this statement: home. I said well, that's real descriptive as he usually is. LOL!! I reply, what happened? And of the two children, the one that is usually less responsive, responds back right away, did you buy a new home, Dad? They never received a response.

I remained close to my former in-laws. They were very good to me and my children. Very occasionally, I happen to meet up with one and have dinner. We were discussing things; the subject of my former spouse came up. I flat out asked how's he doing? The reply was, have you heard? I said I am not sure where you're going, but nothing would surprise me. They proceed to say that he sent them a group text with a picture of a home and indicated that he and his current girlfriend (remember the one that attends my church?) are moving in together. I do not know if they are buying the home together, but they are definitely moving in together. Now, have you been keeping count? What number is this? We have been split 19 and a half years and he is on his third one after me. Like I said before, I guess it wasn't all my fault. LOL.

CHAPTER 21

APRIL 2023

MY FOOT

Well friends, it's been a minute since I've come back to write this book. I wish I could just block out that whole month of April, but sometimes we can't do that. Let me tell you what happened to me.

I think I am still not accustomed to cooking only for one or especially buying produce for one person. I think my young adult children are still here. LOL. Therefore, the produce in the plastic bag in the vegetable drawer of the fridge becomes rotten because I can't eat it all.

On a Thursday evening the first week in April, I decided to clean out the refrigerator. First, I start with the door with all the shelves, take everything off. You know how it is. Then, I proceed shelf by shelf to clean out the main area of the refrigerator. I get to the last shelf, which has a rectangular glass pane on top of the vegetable bin. Cleaned it, dried it, put it back on the shelf that slides back in. As I looked up, my thumbs were gripping this bin. Somehow, the rectangular pane slips off, the point went into my left foot, and no, the glass did not break. My foot stopped it. I proceed to clean my foot, which barely bled. I apply Neosporin and place a band-aid on it!

Every morning out of the shower, I proceed to apply Neosporin and put a new Band-Aid on it. A week later, I get up to let the dog out and I almost fall when I get out of bed. I cannot put weight on my left foot. I hopped down the stairs to the main level, hook the dog up, and sit down a minute. I manage to hop down to the basement steps where I knew my daughter's crutches were. Then, I hop back up, let the dog in. I proceed to sit down for a minute. I said to myself, something is definitely wrong!! I managed to hop and limp to the powder room, grab the door frame, and slide down to the floor. Then I passed out momentarily. I crawled to the toilet, I thought I'm going to die here. I looked down at my nightgown and I'm completely soaked in my sweat. This was no hot flash for menopause!! Once again, I get myself together, grab the crutches, and proceed to go butt-first to the bedroom level.

I grab a quick shower not putting any weight on my left foot. I am holding it up because I'm in tremendous pain!! I'm hopping all around with a crutch. I get dressed. I managed to take two team calls for work. Imagine that!! I get in the car, and I drive to the local Expresscare, which is closest to my home. It's probably within 3 1/2 miles. There are no cars in the parking lot, and I look up the hours of operation on my phone. It doesn't open till 9:00 a.m. and it's only 8:05 a.m. I proceed to read text upon text while elevating my foot on the dashboard. They finally open, and tell me the X-ray machine is broken. I nearly broke down in tears.

I then called Patient First, spoke to a nurse, explained my situation, and asked if their X-ray machine was operable. I was reassured it was and I went on my way. They immediately register me and take me back for X-rays. I continue to keep my foot elevated. They didn't have an exam room available because they were overloaded with flu, not COVID patients!! Finally, I make it to an exam room. More time goes by, a physician's assistant comes in. He says, "I don't think it's broken." I told him, I really don't think so either, I wouldn't be able to walk on it. He asked how I got this injury. I told him about the dear old refrigerator cleaning incident. LOL! He then proceeds to tell me that my foot is infected. I have a puncture wound injury. They gave me a tetanus shot, gave me an antibiotic, amoxicillin, which were like horse pills. I went on my way. I am in tremendous pain still.

I make it home; I proceed to work. I must sleep on this main level because I have a dog that needs to be let out. Naturally, the dog got tangled in a shrub. Then, he got tangled in a tree far away. Thank goodness for my neighbors, Sam, and Sandy, who are wonderful people!! They helped me so much. I am forever grateful for them.

That all occurred on a Friday. Saturday, the next day, I lay low. A very dear friend, Rhonda, stopped over with pizza and a salad, and we chatted. I was in good spirits. Whenever we are together, I laugh!! I was in some discomfort, but it was not awful. I knew the antibiotic was working. I kept soaking my foot, three times a day in warm water to draw out the infection. Isn't that lovely?!

On Sunday, my foot is even more swollen! It is red all the way up to my ankle. I call over my next-door neighbor, Sandy. She says, something is definitely wrong!! She brought over an old people's seat that you sit in the shower with and stayed. She didn't want me to pass out again, as I desperately needed a shower. I then threw on clothes and she helped me get downstairs. I sat in the kitchen until she was able to return. Sure enough, at 10:00 a.m., I was getting in her car to go to the ER. Have I mentioned that I hate hospitals? I know they are there to help. I just don't like them.

We arrive, and she parks on the emergency lane loop so she can put me in a wheelchair; that way I wouldn't have to put my foot down with the crutches. We go into the ER, they take my information, and we proceed to wait. What else do you do in an ER? They take my blood, multiple vials, and even prep me for a pic line. Keep in mind... I'm sitting in a wheelchair with my left leg on another chair. Everybody's walking by, staring at my foot. Afterwards, when I showed the picture to someone in my family, they said it looked like I had a club foot—just so you get the visual of how very swollen it was!

After about an hour and a half, I have to use the restroom. Sandy wheels me into the ladies' room and another person is there. I managed to use the facility and this person says, "Oh my goodness, that looks like very bad cellulitis with MRSA! Oh you're going to be admitted!" Now, folks, have I mentioned I don't like hospitals? I am scared, in pain, my foot and now, leg are becoming more swollen. To top it off, strangers are giving me their medical opinion. WTH?

About an hour after that, another stranger walks by and says that's gotten worse since you've been here! Well at this time, you did not have to wear masks in hospital. How come I chose to wear mine? My neighbor is a cancer survivor. Regardless, these people could not see me and what I was thinking. Did I say it underneath my mask? I was thinking of two choice words starting with F Y. Just saying...

I finally am seen by an ER doctor. He looks at the second set of X-rays I've got done. Again, it is determined that nothing is broken.

You do know you have like something of 52 bones in your foot?! All is good there!!

He says you don't have to be admitted. You do have a very bad case of cellulitis. For those of you who don't know, that is a skin infection; so, basically the puncture wound infection gave me another infection. Guess what? Another antibiotic of Bactrim that I have taken before for sinus infections. I thought for sure, as well as my neighbor, that they would give me an antibiotic IV and that would remedy this situation much more expeditiously. After spending four and half hours there, I come home, and my wonderful neighbors picked up my antibiotic. The pain medication they gave me in the hospital wore off after six hours and I could only take over-the-counter ibuprofen. SHOOT!! The pain kicked in full force.

I'm sleeping in the family room with pain in my foot, it's elevated with about four pillows. I'm only making it upstairs to take a shower every third day because I cannot put any weight anywhere near that foot. I am in too much pain when it is down. By the third day, the antibiotic finally kicked in, I was not in as much pain, I was sleeping four hours at a stretch. This entire time, I was still working from home, per a mandate from the doctors, and working about nine hours a day. I would take a nap after I ate dinner because I was so worn out. I had my neighbors, girlfriends, and family all bring me dinner. I couldn't stand up to make anything due to the pain. I needed to eat because the antibiotics were killing my stomach, and I just kept eating. I'm so grateful for everyone. I was quite scared!

Another girlfriend brought me dinner on Tuesday, five days after the original episode at the urgent care. She looks at my foot and says she doesn't like the looks of something. The swelling has gone down dramatically. However, I developed this tremendous bruising. It's like blood underneath the skin. I even asked about it at the ER. The ER doctor told me not to worry about it, and that it was just inflammation.

Well, I proceeded to call a nurse at CVS, The Minute Clinic. I'm starting to get upset because my neighbor came over and said, oh you really should call someone as well. Come to find out, it's all because of the pressure and it got swollen. The blood went to the lowest part (i.e. gravity) and when I'm elevating it, the blood pools underneath my ankle by the bottom of my foot. It was pure ugly!! Just keep it elevated and rest because it was too late for ice!

By this time, I am so very sick of talking to any medical professional as you can imagine!! I proceeded to work from home for the next two weeks. My GP (general practitioner) requested that I take a picture of my foot every other day and upload it. She would not release me to go back to work until she saw me in person. I do understand that. I went to see her after two and a half weeks of being home. That seemed forever when you're waiting for something to heal, you can't walk, you were in pain, and you have terrible bruising. Especially if you want to take a shower daily.

In the meantime, I'm still on Match.com!! Each night, I kept hitting that Discover button to see what I would discover!! Can I say not much? I began corresponding with a gentleman named Tom from a town about an hour away. His city is on the water and known for boating, great restaurants, and spectacular views.

After many emails, we exchanged phone numbers, and we talked quite a bit on the phone. He is in sales for a pool company up and down the East Coast. He has four children from two separate marriages. He was very anxious to meet. He called me last minute and suggested he come up my way to have lunch. He claimed he was in the area. I met him using one crutch at a Mexican restaurant, we chatted a bit, had a great lunch. As usual, I offered to split the bill and he said no. I offered to leave tip, he said no again. I'm sure he put it on his company credit card.

We were talking about traveling to possible destinations. My children and I were headed on a vacation the following month, about five weeks away. He said he would never go there. We were talking about children, and he asked me what mine was studying. I told him. When I explained what my daughter does for a living, with environmental science, he says I really don't believe companies really take heed and follow the rules. He was very opinionated on all these subjects. Slowly, I stopped asking questions, we were wrapping up lunch, and both of us had to get back to work. I thanked him for lunch and he walked me to my car.

We spoke a few times after that. I was off crutches by then. On a Thursday night, he texts me to ask me to his home on a Saturday night. Keep in mind that we have only had one date. I asked him, don't you have your two daughters this weekend? He responds, "I just want to see if there was chemistry between us." I reply, "Well we've emailed a lot; we went to lunch, we're talking on the phone." Then, he says, not that kind of chemistry, more like physical chemistry. I replied, "I just met you."

Now ladies, I'm not saying there couldn't have been more chemistry. I'm just not that way. Can we have more than one date to get to know each other? And he was so opinionated. It made me shut down. I mean I would have respected him more if he came out and said I want a booty call. He might as well have!

Now gentlemen, are you freaking kidding me? One lunch date and that is it? I'm not saying I have to be wined and dined. But a Mexican lunch for a little over an hour AND I know he charged it to his company credit card. I don't get this. Virtually, we're all strangers through this online maze of dating. No one knows anybody through anybody or anything else. I certainly do not want to catch anything! I mean I'm not judging here, men or women. That's not my point. For those of us who don't want to partake in those activities after the first, second, or third date, don't get mad. Everyone has a different comfort zone. Everyone needs to feel safe. Bottom line: I wasn't feeling it for a multitude of reasons.

We all know that men want the physical part first and women want the emotional part first. What do we do as a society when this occurs? Anyway, the guy never called me back after that. Not sure where I went wrong? Or if I really did? Feel free to weigh in and e-mail me your thoughts. I'm always up for a good conversation.

Lesson: Both men and women be upfront, tell the other what you want. If this gentleman just wanted a roll in the hay, fine. BE transparent.

CHAPTER 22

SPRING TO SUMMER 2023

The month of April was finally over. I went back to work each day. I still could not do much activity. I could at least cook for myself and stand a little. I went out, bought compression socks, and wore them for a bit. Ironically and much to my surprise, it was helping. I also elevated my foot underneath my desk at work.

The month of May was pretty much a blur. The first two weeks I was still recovering, slowly getting around. I didn't go out much at all. I went back to my night shift job on Friday nights. Then, the third week in May, my son graduated from college and those were a whirlwind few days. I went back to work for a few days, then both of my children and I left for a five-day family vacation postponed for three years (due to COVID) to Mexico! Vacation was a blast! It was much needed and well-deserved by all.

There were no more dates in May as it was a hectic month, and I was recovering at the beginning of the month. Every night, I did hit that Discover button on Match.com. Nothing proved interesting enough to meet. I kept trying. Each day, I am praying. Maybe I should give up and realize that this is my path, to be completely single?

In this process, I kept busy. I was taking care of me!!! I went forth in my career, raised two young adults, and started to enjoy my favorite season, summer. It's my time now. A girlfriend told me when I turned 5o, that it was my turn. I waited until both children graduated from college.

CHAPTER 23

JUNE 2023

The month of May flew by, and my foot continues to improve. The bruising was still there. I went to a podiatrist, and he stated it could take three months from the time he saw me for both the swelling to go down and the bruising to dissipate.

In the beginning of June, I met the eleventh gentleman from Match.com. Stan from New Jersey, had a great job, was about to turn 60, had two children, a boy and a girl younger than mine. He seemed funny, smart, and a great guy to talk to. He suggested we meet halfway. I had no problem with that. He suggested meeting at a Starbucks for a coffee. Imagine that!!! Isn't that the ole standby, guys? Let's meet for a coffee. It's quick and easy! Then, we will find out if she is quick and easy and worth the time to have dinner with? Come on, it may sound cynical, but I call it like I see it. Truly, I do.

I drive 40 miles from my home to meet him at the Starbucks in Christiana Mall, Delaware. I meet him, he is better looking in person, I must admit. He is very tall. The world is tall compared to me as I am only 5"1. LOL! Seriously, he is over 6 foot. We have a great conversation; he brought me a yellow rose. It was a very nice gesture. And no, I didn't feel like I was on the Bachelor TV show! LOL. I didn't have to earn that rose! I crack myself up! Regardless, it was a super sweet gesture.

We parted after almost two hours; he walked me to my car. He asked that I let him know when I made it home, which I did. He proceeded to stay in touch every day. He texted, 'Good Morning' religiously. This dialogue continued for about six weeks. Then, one day, I was extremely busy, didn't return his text, and the GM texts stopped just like that. Isn't that interesting? He never asked me out again at all. Only sent the 'Good Morning texts.' I guess I gave him an out.

The kicker is... he never called me in between, never suggested meeting again, nothing. He just wasn't that into me. Like would it really work any way being two hours apart geographically? Would it work with his kids coming and going between his place and their mother's with no schedule? He also seems to spoil his kids tremendously. You may think that I am being negative or super particular. You just have to at least think about these things if you want a serious relationship. I can tell he wasn't that serious.

Lesson: Do not meet up with someone if they are outside your commute zone, meaning, in my case, 4o miles to meet for a cup of coffee wasn't it for me.

I want someone that wants me, doesn't need me, but wants me. I might also add—they don't want me for that one thing. You know what I mean! No, friends with benefits (FWB) or f___ buddies (FB) here, no way! I deserve more, and I will get it. Even if I do not find my mate, I will not settle. I have come to terms with God's plan for my life. I may die alone and be forever alone. I accept that. It's all in His plan and we shall see. However, I am spiritual and believe. Many of my faith-filled friends say God would not have put that ideal in your heart if it wasn't meant to happen, and if I was meant to be alone. So have faith, I will!

About mid-June, I meet the twelfth gentleman from Match.com. We conversed over email, he seemed pleasant, had a job in accounting, was physically active, but... You know there is always a BUT! He is only separated, not divorced. I swore I would never date a separated-only guy again. I had been hurt too many times! Things must be done logistically, and even more so emotionally, where it counts!

This gentleman, Mark, suggested a very nice place to meet at 5:30 p.m. for a beverage. We met on a Wednesday evening, and no one was at the bar, but the two of us. I ordered a glass of pinot grigio and he had a Manhattan. We sat and chatted for a bit, quite an interesting guy, with a deep faith. We also had quite a few things in common. As the conversation went on, he was talking with his hands. I do the same thing! He was sitting to my left and I could not see his left hand too clearly. Finally, I see it and he is still sporting a plain gold wedding band. WTH?! It creeped me out. Truly, it did! I finished my glass of wine, he asked if I would like another, or something else. I replied no. Then, he did ask if I wanted to get a bite to eat there. Now, that was tempting! The food there is delicious from presentation to taste, worth it! I replied I had to go and that was that.

The next day I received a text from him stating how good it was to meet me, he enjoyed himself, and could we get together again? I replied, it was nice meeting you. However, I was slightly taken back when I saw you wear your wedding band. He proceeded to explain via text that he is sorry it made me uncomfortable. Since he has a deep faith and his religion is important to him, he will continue to wear his wedding band as he is still married in the eyes of God's covenant and legally. Can I just say WOW? Let me say it again—WOW!

He also called to apologize, stating, he didn't mean for it to be awkward or uncomfortable. If I am that uncomfortable with it, perhaps we can re-connect after he gets divorced? I replied, yes, that would be better. Did I mention that he was also on his third marriage? Some people cannot be alone.

While I see his point about still being married and respect it, that does not mean I understand. Let me give a little bit of background here... he asked me to go hiking which, while I love to do, I could not because of my foot injury. He also invited me to the movies with him. However, I didn't read the email message via the Match website until after the time of the movie. He did not give sufficient notice. My point is... he invited me on three outings. I was only available for one. I am confused because it's ok to date while still wearing your wedding band? Help me out with this please! I won't disclose the views of a few of my girlfriends. Thoughts? I welcome them. Please feel free to reach out.

Lesson to all: If you want to date, why still wear your wedding band if it's over? If the eyes of your higher being or not, isn't that like an oxymoron? Really?

CHAPTER 24

THE LAST FEW WEEKS OF THE SUBSCRIPTION

It's mid-June 2023 and I have only a few weeks left of my subscription of Match.com. I have met twelve men so far, and some have been better than others, needless to say. I am thinking to myself that I could attempt to meet one more guy. You never know, this could be the one!! Right?!! It's like playing the lottery... you never know you could buy the lucky ticket!!! LOL.

A gentleman reached out to me first. He was really attractive, gray hair, almost white actually, sharp dresser, seemed like he had a sense of humor in his write-up. He seemed to be intelligent also. After exchanging a few emails via the site back and forth, he asked me for my phone number after he presented his. He called me a few times, we spoke at length, had enough in common for sufficient dialogue to keep the conversation going. Here is one negative, but I had to get over it. He has the same first name as my former spouse. Not all men with that name are bad, right?! Maybe it was me? It is just a name. I am going to step out of my comfort zone and be positive!

He lived about 45 minutes away from me. What the heck??? It's for love, right? Why not meet him, see what happens? You never know, as they say.

On the first date, we agreed to meet at a place about a 30-minute commute for each of us. That was good, halfway for each of us. No one goes too far out of the way. He suggested we meet at this nice restaurant attached at the end of this mall, a steakhouse and grille of sorts. It was about the third week in June and for the East Coast in Maryland, it was a rather chilly day with a high of 65 degrees. He even called me when I was very close and told me what floor he parked on so we could walk in together. I thought that was very considerate. I proceed to park on that level and meet him. Well, he was dressed nice which is hard to find!

It wasn't anything spectacular, but he presented well. He put on a button-down collar shirt untucked, with decent jeans, and loafers.

We proceed to the restaurant and are seated at a booth; I order a glass of pinot grigio and he follows my lead. I order the steak salad, and he orders the salmon with broccoli and mashed potatoes. My steak salad was excellent. It was more than just your average salad with filet mignon tips on top. Decadent, indeed. He enjoyed his salmon as well. We sat there for almost two hours talking, we each only had one glass of wine. I will admit I could have had another while we talked, but I didn't. The weather on this evening was awful, rainy, cold, dreary, miserable, and terrible to drive in. One glass of wine was enough indeed.

After dinner, we were walking to the garage where we parked on the same level. He then tells me come to his car. I asked, why? He says he just wants to sit and talk. Quickly, I texted a girlfriend... sitting in his car now. You know, just in case something happens, and I end up chopped up somewhere. There were enough people around though, coming and going.

He takes me to his car, and it is quite the car. We had conversations about cars because he is very into cars as he is a former race car driver! Really, who would have thought? I must say I think that is one profession of a gentleman that I hadn't yet dated! LOL. We talk about a number of things, we listen to the radio, then I insisted that I must be getting home—it was getting late, I was tired, still drizzling. We parted ways with a hug and a kiss on the cheek, and I texted him when I got home as he asked.

We spoke a few times on the phone, and he asked me out on a second date. YAHOO! The second time, we met in the same area as it was convenient for both of us. This time he suggested Mexican, fine. I meet him and this time he wasn't dressed as nice. Though, he wore a golf shirt, it was a little tight around the middle, if you know what I mean. While I understand we are all getting older, do NOT claim you are active all the time per your dating profile. We have a very good Mexican dinner, each having a margarita. I ordered a skinny margarita, thinking someone would take the hint and they did not. LOL. I talk about how I work out, walk at the very least while also working two jobs. They work remotely from home. They take the dog on a walk, but that is it. No cardio, no crunches. Just saying!

I hate to say the second date wasn't as much fun as the first. I thought it was timing or moods or something. It happens. Who knows? We finish our Mexican meal in an hour, and I could tell he didn't want to end the date. By the way, he did pay for the dates. Though, I did offer to split it or tip and he declined for both dates.

The movie theater was across the street, so we venture there. I had no idea of a movie in mind. I thought we would take a walk or grab a drink and chat. We go to the movies and as it was summer, there were many animated movies showing. Long story short, he checks his watch and quickly states we can see "Asteroid City." I say ok, I had no idea who was in it. We saw posters advertising it and it seems to have many well-known actors in it. Well, let me just tell you. DO not watch this movie unless you need to cure insomnia for an evening. Truly, this is a sleeper. It had Tom Hanks, Scarlett Johannsen, and Steve Farrell with roles. This movie is portrayed in Acts and Scenes as in a play, which is fine. However, there really is no true plot, theme, or storyline. It's terrible! Let me tell you how it captures the audience. He fell asleep twice and I nudged him with my elbow awake.

That was only after he kept answering texts from his 19-year-old daughter. I am a parent and I get it. He has her one week on, and one week off. She just didn't text she was home. She was asking when he was coming home and everything else. Finally, we made it through the movie, we are in the parking garage, and I said let's pay this now rather than at the machine exiting the garage. He claims we don't have to pay it. OMG. No, we do!! He drives me to my car when I can walk. Keep in mind—it's 11 p.m. now. I am tired, we met at 7 p.m. and I have to work the next day. I must drive minimally 30 minutes home, let the dog out, and get ready for bed. He wants to hang out by my car, and I say I just want to get home. Finally, we exit the parking garage in each of our cars and he doesn't think you have to pay for parking, remember? Guess what? You HAVE TO PAY FOR PARKING! I do that, pull out on the road, and head home. It took almost 45 minutes as there was construction on a major highway on my way home. I let the dog out, got ready for bed, and crawled into bed at midnight. UGH!

In hindsight, I should have looked at the run time of the movie. I really thought we would just walk around or go somewhere else to chat. In the movie, I told him we are not acting like we are 16 or 18-year-olds in the movie. I could just tell where he was headed, and I put the brakes on that pronto!!!

He went away, we were both busy, and we didn't see each other for about 12 days. He called me on a Sunday afternoon, coming home from a trip where he raced. He invited me on this trip, and I said it was way too soon, told him I didn't have much leave for vacation, blah, blah, blah. He wasn't supposed to come home until Monday, but he hardly raced due to car troubles and came home early. He asked what I was doing later, I explained I was going to a girlfriend's mother's viewing. He asked me to come over. Now, ladies, I normally never do this. Believe me, I made the rules clear, NOTHING IS HAPPENING.

I head to his home after the viewing. I am about five minutes away from his home. Remember that! We don't talk 30 seconds and he says, oh, that's my daughter calling, I have to go. The world stops for his daughter. Truly, he has not taught her any independence. I arrive, he gives me a tour of his home, including the practice area for his band and his race simulator. LOL. He introduces me to the dog, and has her demonstrate the dog tricks. Then, we watch race cars flying around a track and I ask questions. Now, it's not the most exciting thing. It seems he doesn't want to talk, but he'd rather be Mr. Octopus and his hands are trying to touch me. I stopped once, twice, and I said, please don't make me smack you. Then, he is hungry, he proceeds to eat an apple in front of me and says want any? I said no, thank you. He is starving, I told him you could have called, and I could have picked something up. He says I will just wait til you go. So far, I was only there a half hour. We watched the end of this race. Thank goodness, it ended, and I stated I was heading home. I was on my way. I stayed an hour.

Let's review a few things. He never ate apparently, he didn't offer me a glass of wine, water, nothing. Get this? He had bottles of water on the counter. He was like Mr. Octopus. He says, "Wouldn't it be great if he went in my bedroom right now?" I emphatically said NO!

Really? I told you prior. I was very much put off. I proceeded on my way home, which took me 53 minutes from his house. There was construction on Interstate 95, I let the dog out, got ready for bed, and it was almost 11:30 p.m. He never told me to text hi, when I get home, or anything. He didn't make sure I made it home. That was it.

When I woke up the next morning, I see a picture sent by him around 12:45 a.m. of the dog's head on my lap. So, you send this picture, but couldn't say I hope you made it home fine? Later in the day, I receive a text stating, "Thanks for seeing my home and visiting me." I replied back, "Cute picture of the dog. Thought you would have made sure I made it home?" He replies, "You were supposed to let me know." I was? I replied, "I didn't hear you say that."

A couple of days go by, and a few texts go back and forth. On a Wednesday evening at 5:40 p.m., I am still at work. I happen to be having an evening conference call, which rarely happens that late in the day. He texts me, "How are you doing today? What are you doing this evening?" I explained I was still at work on a conference call, heading home to exercise, do things around the house. That response prompted, "Want me to get carry out and come over?" I did not say emphatically NO! I thought it though. LOL! After consulting a girlfriend, I suggested we meet halfway like we did twice prior. It was 5:55 p.m. and I am pulling out of where I work, suggested we aim for 7-7:30 p.m. like before. While I am driving, I am thinking about what I can change into quickly while the dog is outside, I feed him, etc.

He texts while I am driving let's meet at the same area we met before. I reply, ok, fine. Then, another text comes in which states three location spots as in areas (not establishments) we can meet and he describes the time it takes for him to get to each area. Now, I am blonde, but not that blonde as I say! He and I both grew up in the same state, maybe 4o minutes apart. I know those areas and can figure it out. After suggesting coming to my home, he picks the restaurant CLOSEST to him and FURTHEST for me! Really? Can we say he is not HV as in a high-value man? Forget going out of his way, he won't even do halfway.

I get in my car to be on my way to the FURTHEST area out of the three he chose, and I need gas. I probably could have made it there, but I definitely could not have made it home. I get gas close to my home, where it's more convenient for me, slightly cheaper, and then, I will be on my way. He texts while I am en route, stating where he is sitting at the restaurant. I did not have the directional map app up on my phone because I knew where the restaurant was, was on my way, and there you have it. I have told him I was going to be about 10 minutes late due to getting gas. Keep in mind this was all spur of the moment!

He calls me while I am driving and I couldn't reach the phone in my purse, then I talk to text stating was less than 15 minutes away. He proceeds to write back, stating he is leaving. I talk to text back, "Really? This came about last minute. I told you I had to let the dog out, and I needed gas." He writes, "When you date, let people know you are going to be late." I called him back immediately, which he did not answer. I, then, talked to text stating: "1) this whole date was very last minute, 2) you chose the place CLOSEST to yourself, 3) I told him I needed gas, 4) you can't wait 15 minutes for me? WTH? Really?"

Can you say DONE?!!! So very done!! I mean I am not going back to online dating again... I am not. He is not worth my time and no one like him! I rather be by myself, stay single, etc.

Lesson: A guy may appear great, but take heed, ladies. I will never meet a guy last minute again, ever.

CHAPTER 25

LAYOFF

July was not a great month unfortunately. Stuff happens! First, my birthday is the beginning of the month. Ugh another year older and time stops for no one, as they say. Where did the year go? I don't feel older really. Though, the foot incident aged me. I really believe online dating has aged me also. Imagine that!!

Second, I stopped dating, online or anyone else. Just done! More than over it. Tired of the aggravation, effort, low-value men, and general BS! It's extremely draining. Besides that, I felt it was time to concentrate on myself. I must find a job ASAP! You'll find out why below!

The summer is flying by as it usually does. Summer is my favorite season! It is also one of my busiest months for work, as there are not only monthly deliverables due, but quarterly ones as well. I also assisted with a proposal my employer was bidding on and prepared slides for an internal program management review (PMR). I was called in less than 30 minutes before this PMR and was laid off. Talk about blindsided, that I was! Ironically, I had updated my resume and begun looking for a position a few weeks prior. Sometimes, you just know your worth. I certainly was not appreciated. I did so many tasks for this company, such as streamlined processes, mentored individuals, assisted with proposals, brought in homemade brunches, and bought plants for the lobby to make the place more inviting. All these simple, but detailed, thoughtful tasks. I constantly thought of ways for improvement, efficiencies, and risk mitigation. I mentored risk mitigation and corrected multiple problems. I just don't understand. Truly, I don't comprehend the goals of the small business contractors for the government. They think they are invincible, and you are trying to guide and lead them.

This occurred the last week in July 2023. I had a pity party for half a day, then got to work the last two days of the week. I set up a few more job searches, and the hunt began! I was determined, and disgusted. I went from stress eating to eating super healthy and doing abs exercises twice a day. Can I just say being laid off is no fun? It's extremely stressful. The money you were accustomed to is not coming in. Not that I EVER spent my whole paycheck in the last ten years. I save incredibly well and thank goodness that I do! Needless to say, a major repair was needed. It always happens at the most inconvenient time! The hot water heater went up. UGH! Now, I know it's summer and a number of people have said, Well, at least it's summer. You know what? You still need hot water. Have you ever tried to rinse the conditioner out of your hair with cold or even tepid water? It just doesn't work, just saying. Just picture that!

I had two planned weekends away in August. The first weekend away was with the girlfriends in Ocean City, Maryland, for the White Marlin weekend. Nothing like the beach, sunshine, and a party!!! LOL. I was looking for a job before and after I went away. I have a part-time job, which I continued to work, for the last four and half years, the night shift. I still work this job for a number of reasons. 1) They carry my clearance at a higher level. You see, many small defense contracting companies will not maintain an employee's clearance at a higher level. It costs money and they don't want to front it. I get it, but it does help my career. So, I keep working this part-time job to maintain a higher level of clearance. Thank goodness and I am forever grateful for this part-time job!! 2) I love, just love, the company that holds my clearance. This job has saved me, it has kept me afloat! It pays more than unemployment. Unfortunately, it only pays about one-third of my full-time job. Nonetheless, I am so fortunate and blessed that this company has allowed me to work hours. It's more money than unemployment, I maintain my higher clearance, I get out of the house and feel semi-productive. It's a win!! God is always good!!

Everything happens for a reason. I truly believe this! Do you? Stop and think about it... haven't things happened in your life, and everything works out? Actually, things DO work out for the better! There is a BIGGER AND BETTER PLAN when events like this happen. You have to believe it! And, if another person tells me—when one door closes, a window opens, I WILL SCREAM!!! My comeback is... the window is smaller. LOL! Just kidding, just kidding. In all seriousness, I am taking deep breaths, meditating, looking for the signs. It's all part of God's plan, but I have to tell you right here and now, at this very moment, I HAVE NO CLUE ABOUT GOD'S PLAN FOR MY LIFE. Regardless, you must trust in Him, especially if you are born and raised Catholic. We believe, we believe, and we believe some more, even when all the odds are against us.

At this chapter, I have been unemployed for six weeks now. I feel like 'The Little Train That Could.' Remember that story we read to our children? Instead of, I think I can, I think I can... I say I know I can. I know I can. It's going to happen, that's what I say! I know it will. It's timing and patience. I am Irish, but I have no Irish luck!! So, timing is not on my side, and I am not the most patient person.

Lesson: Be patient with many things. Most importantly, be patient with yourself. Work on yourself, in this instance, professionally. Keep your confidence up and don't give up.

CHAPTER 26

THE FUNNEL

(CIRCULAR DATING)

Here, I am in my mid-5os, ahem, and unemployed. Now, who is going to want that? Let me recap... the Match subscription ended at the beginning of July. I have no desire to date, I am not in my best state of mind, nor am I looking my best because I have worry lines engraved in my face!! Can I tell you... it is true when you are NOT looking, you meet people?

I have a male friend, Phillip, who I have known for many years, and he has done a number of renovations and repairs on my home. We are very, very good friends. In fact, like 10 years ago, we went out for like 22 minutes. Just kidding, we went out just a few times. Timing wasn't on our side. It happens.

There always seems to be that one parent from a divorced situation that takes over the responsibilities. The other parent has stepped away, so the one parent must step up. That's what we do! The kids have suffered enough. Phillip and I have both been through a lot in our own journeys—raising kids; I concentrated on my career with getting an advanced degree and certification, and he owns his own business. He also started a second business. We have this on again/off again hang out and watch movie night. He is just a friend. We hang out, talk, watch movies, and have a drink. That's it. Then, he lights up my phone with texts multiple days a week. This was happening way before I got laid off. Suddenly, I get laid off, and the texts subsided too. Imagine that! I will leave that up to you to form your opinion. Just saying...

For years, I have wanted to join a yacht club that 3.5 miles from my home. No, I don't own a boat. The view is spectacular!!! I have a social and pool membership since I love hanging out at the pool. The people are so welcoming and personable. Well, it's just too cute! I love it there!!! The people are so friendly and welcoming. It is very reasonably priced because the members must complete volunteer hours. It helps with outgoing costs. One day, they put out a request for 'help needed' blowing leaves a day before a big party. No problem. I volunteered. I arrived in a scoop neck casual dress right from the part-time job. I had a blazer over my dress at work, so I was fine. I arrive and start blowing leaves, all is well. Then, another male club member, Tim, shows up with his teenage children to help him because he needs his volunteer hours. Those three are executing other yardwork chores. I finish blowing the leaves, which wasn't that bad, and next thing I know, Tim, brought his OWN leaf blower. He just had to go behind me and make sure everything was just so! Really? Oh, my goodness. These men have to show you they are it! They do. He does that, I laugh over it, and leave. All is well.

I run two errands, go home, eat dinner, and review the job searches. I go onto my night shift job that is oh-so-exciting, but it still pays the bills. Thank goodness. The next morning, I have my routine and get going. I check my phone I see an instant message on Facebook from Tim. WTH? This is odd. I proceed to read, "Thanks for letting me help you with the leaves. You were the best dressed one there."

Again, are you serious? You can't make this up! For real, like a guy looked me up in less than 24 hours, than messaged me. Wow, like that will never happen again! After the shock wore off and I had coffee, I messaged him back. This banter continued a bit over the weekend. Slowly, we were instant messaging each other back and forth. He asked where I worked, and I mentioned buildings where I USED to work on the local army base. Guess what? Go ahead and say it. He works there too! He is a big whig!!! He is a Chief so now, I call him that, and now Tim. LOL! We bantered back and forth, and I explained I was laid off from my full-time job and am working my part-time job until I find one. I must say this is extremely embarrassing... telling a guy you just met that you got laid off, especially with experience, a master's degree, and PMP certification. He was okay with it. We kind of made a joke out of it.

It has been over three weeks, and he has not asked me out for coffee or a drink! He did ask me once on a Thursday night if I was at the yacht club, it was 9 p.m. I was not, as I was getting ready for a last-minute night shift. Quite frankly, he asked me very last minute as well. I could not make it. In fairness, he does have his teenage children on a week and off a week. Still, a little planning would be nice! Just saying...

Let me tell you his positive attributes... he is average height, very intelligent, good-looking, funny, and he happens to be six years younger. Now, I hardly ever date younger men. EVER! I am just way too mature, have my crap together. And they don't. His kids are still teenagers, a daughter who is a senior in high school and a son who is a sophomore in high school. Let's see if I hear from him or he is too busy or a flirt. I am not betting on it!!

Lesson for women primarily: Just because men give you attention and text back and forth, are playful, look you up, does not mean they are interested long-term. You merely grabbed their attention. Nothing is permanent or definite.

CHAPTER 27

LOOKING FOR EMPLOYMENT,

AND THEN SOME

August rolled into September. I have been working my part time night shift job but for the day shifts. Those extra shifts paid the bills... Barely, that is. I didn't have to file for unemployment. So, I saved that company money. I did that for about eight weeks. I was living off of savings that I had accumulated in my account. Thank the Lord I did not have to go into my investments. Nonetheless, I couldn't use it on renovations for the house, which I wanted to and had been saving for. Instead, I was using it to live off of.

Let me tell you how God works. Just when you think you're at your lowest low and things can get much worse, you get a sign. I truly believe in signs!! On one particular night in August, actually it was the first Friday in August, I get text messages from former coworkers they are at a bar on Main Street in the county where I live because of karaoke. Someone left the company; it was a going away party; 'Come up and do karaoke,' the text said. Well, I thought I really don't feel like going out. I thought I'd go out just for one beer. I was sitting here in lounge clothes on a summer evening, meaning not planning on going out. I decided to change clothes, brush my hair, and put on a tad more mascara. Usually, as I'm so petite at 5 foot one, I wear heels all the time. I chose to wear flip flops with like an inch wedge. I drive up there, walk into the establishment, and see the gang.

What happens next? I see Lee, a guy I dated 13 years ago for like only four dates. I try not to take it personally, I mean 13 years ago was a long time. We didn't date that long; we had a great time when we went out! He's tall, in great shape, has gorgeous, piercing blue eyes and they are intense in a good way. His smile is unbelievable!! Can I say perfect straight white teeth as well?! He never wore braces, and it just kills me because I did and still wear a retainer.

Did I mention he doesn't have any hair? Ohhhh, but he is a hot baldy!! Yes indeed!

I couldn't believe my eyes! He looked at me and I looked at him, and then he said, "Hi how are you?" I think I saw him like a year and a half ago maybe? Just around Bel Air in passing and waved. I wasn't mad, we didn't date long. Nothing happened, you talk about a true gentleman. He is!! One-of-a-kind in today's world and I know that. I knew it back then too!! Never forgot that!! He proceeds to ask me to stand near him, and we talk. I try to inch away and he's like, no hang out at my table, which was only like six feet away from my other table of my former coworkers. We hung out, he asked me if I wanted to drink, and I said, I'll just take one beer. I tried to pay him, he said no. He was so attentive and kept looking at me and here I looked and felt like I was a total bum! I really wasn't, but I was a little bit casual and like I don't care.

He started the conversation, asked me how I was doing, I filled him in, but I didn't say I was laid off, that night. I was there for about two hours and said hi to his friends who I knew from the first time all those years ago. He insisted upon walking me to my car and I kept saying no, no, no. In hindsight, that's the best thing he ever did for me!! He walked me to my car that night! He was a complete gentleman, his mother raised him right! I simply got in my car and left. I texted him when I got home and told him I made it. Said it was great to run into him again, and to stay in touch. He returned my text the next day. He asked if I'd like to have lunch, and I responded, sure. Then, we proceeded to stay in touch for the next few weeks. Unfortunately, I had two weekends planned back-to-back that I was going away. Both of those plans were made way before I got laid off, way way way before. He stayed in touch, and said, no worries.

In the meantime, I'm applying to jobs and applying to jobs and applying to jobs. That's all I was doing as I was working that part-time job. I was not going out or socializing. I was staying in, applying for jobs, drinking at home, and saving money. I had those weekends planned in August. The second weekend in August was with the girlfriends away. The third weekend in August my father rented an Airbnb for my family, my half-sister's family, and my father. It was so much fun!!!

Finally, the last weekend in August arrives. We had made plans to get together then. We ended up going out on the last Sunday of August. We had a blast. He wanted to pick me up and I said let me meet you. He insisted on picking me up. You have to understand that I am totally not used to that because I usually meet men on dating sites. I don't let them anywhere near me. I temporarily forgot he knew where I lived because he picked me up the first time years ago. So, it goes. We went to a lovely place on the water further north from here. It was a little drive, which took about 4o minutes, had lunch, and a few drinks.

Oh, and guess who I run into? Phillip, the gentleman that did contracting work for me. He later told me that guy doesn't seem right for you; you guys have different energy. I love how he could figure all that out from an introduction of two people. What does that take? Two minutes? LOL. Tell me Phillip wasn't keeping his eye on me. He was actually texting me that whole morning and beginning of the afternoon while I was getting ready. WTH? It was all silly banter.

Lesson: Let me repeat—just because a guy or gal texts the other person does not mean they are interested long-term. That is just someone to keep them occupied in the present moment. Someone to banter with, flirt with, and cure boredom!

Lunch ended and he drove me home. I asked if he wanted to come in which he did for about 45 minutes. He stayed in touch, called. It was really something!! We started off very slow. He does live a distance away from me about 45 minutes. He's definitely worth it!! I will say it once and I will say it again, he is. His smile lights up a room, he makes you laugh over silly things.

I've never met a man that made me laugh and smile the way he did, and, in the beginning, I really couldn't tell if he liked me or not. At times, I still can't tell. He was married for over 20 years; his wife ended up having an alcohol problem, and then she cheated on them. Took months for me to find out, that he had her in rehab twice, and he did everything he could for her. However, alcoholism is a disease. People have to help themselves to a point.

Lesson: Both men and women must open up on their own. They have to be vulnerable and ready to open emotionally. Ready for a relationship.

CHAPTER 28

FALL IS APPROACHING

meantime, during the whole month of September, I am filling out job applications, going on interviews, getting offertory letters for contingent positions. That means only if the government contractor wins the award, and it may not be awarded for months. What am I to do? I needed a job like yesterday. I keep paying the bills and going from there. Of course, I stopped shopping. In the middle of all this, in mid-August, my hot water heater goes up. Nothing is simple. I felt very overwhelmed.

However, in the meantime well, Lee kept being positive and that's one of his greatest attributes!! He was a great cheerleader for me. That's when you know you have a great guy!! He kept saying you'll find something, you'll find something, he didn't lose faith, but...I lost faith in myself. It's a horrible thing to have happened to you. And here I am, with the master's degree and my project management professional certification, PMP, without a job.

At the end of September 2023, I accepted a position at another local Army base about an hour away. I was going to be a senior program manager at another military base further away. It was a 90-mile commute round trip. Took an hour in the morning, about an hour and 15 to head home. Ironically, this job was really not that hard, pay was equitable. Though, it took forever to get the proper accesses. Oh, and I say the division that I work for, no one wanted to work? The government points of contact came in once a week and we needed access. Of course, forms were only filled out the ONE day they were in the office. It was extremely slow getting started. I had another person tell me who worked for the small business that this is the way it is; he was micromanaging me, it was unbelievable. In the meantime, I kept filling out applications for the military base closer to home. It was the commute, the gas, had to get someone to let the dog out who was older because it was a long day. I never received a government laptop to work off of until three weeks after I was there.

The absolute only great thing about working at that end of town blah blah blah was that I got to see Lee on Friday evenings after work. It was great! I look so forward to seeing him. It really strengthened that relationship, and we had the start of something good.

Then, I began a job at APG in the third week of November 2023. It was for the best!! I have never, ever not worked a job so little in my life. But I was truly miserable. Can I just say there's a lot of other things to like than money? Yes, it helps!! But there were too many other factors. The work environment made me extremely uncomfortable. I was getting looked at up and down, and it was turning into stares. No one was answering questions, it was an extremely slow process. Can I just say that organization is not what I thought!

My professional life was back on track as I returned to where I was accustomed. I was going in five days a week for the first few weeks, doing lots of tasks, getting things situated, trying to meet all the people that I supervised, which was just under 50 direct reports. I love this job!!! As I write this chapter, I've been there four months. Though, seems like much longer. I acclimated myself very quickly. I had to let a few people go due to funding, I had to let a few others go due to poor performance after putting them on a performance improvement plan (PIP), of course. It's a lot. I'm mentoring people, getting reports narrowed down from 37 pages to 23 pages. Meeting with key contacts of the government. I do love it!! I love my role, the direct reports, the government counterparts. Just everything. I am so blessed!! This is a prayer truly answered and another small miracle. God is good. Always!

In the meantime, I do continue to see Lee. By mid-November, Lee introduced me to one of his three sisters, and his adult son. I had also met two different sets of friends. One he grew up with and has known for almost 40 years. The other couple lives in the town where he lives. Holidays come and go. Thanksgiving comes and rolls into Christmas. I think I never said thank you enough and I never showed enough appreciation. We were having fun getting to know one another!!

Ironically, he was so different from the last guy that I dated. I think I was just in awe. It was surreal. He was truly a gentleman. We were getting to know one another ever so slowly. I sat by myself on Thanksgiving as my young adult children continued to go to their father's side on that day. We celebrate our Thanksgiving the Saturday after. For the first time ever, we went out to a restaurant. We went for a very early dinner, so my daughter could head back to where she lives that evening, and Lee met my children as we were finishing up dinner. It was great! He was laughing and everything. I could tell he was nervous though. He did great and was very engaging.

On Christmas evening, I met the rest of his family, which included another sister, his adult daughter, her husband and the two grandsons. I also met his 80-year-old mother. I had met his son, but now met his girlfriend too. It was great! I felt we were getting somewhere. You don't introduce someone to all these people if it weren't.

Lesson: I want to repeat never take those moments for granted. EVER!

It's heck to be by yourself during the holidays and I should be used to it after 20 years since my children left me and went to the other side. I truly wasn't. It never gets easier. He and I had a date and then he invited me over for Christmas afternoon after my children went to their father's side. I stayed for quite a few hours because I got there mid to late afternoon, and then the Ravens game came on; I left by the third quarter not to overstay. I had to work the next day also, but he didn't.

Now, I must mention I did get him something for Christmas and he did not get me anything. He told me he wouldn't. Some women I know would have extreme trouble with this. I did not. He told me he wasn't; he does not get into Christmas and all the gift-giving. He only gets his two adult children, his grandchildren, and his mother. He doesn't like to go shop blah blah blah blah blah. Now, there is a reason for this. His wife constantly shopped ALL the time for herself. I think he feels women just do it for themselves.

I will admit I wasn't thrilled, but that is not me nor is that what the holiday is about. It's about giving. I get much enjoyment out of giving and not receiving. I was enjoying time with Lee, being around people, seeing how he interacted with his family and vice versa. Actually, seeing how his friends welcomed me, accepting me and so on, was refreshing. It made me feel secure and safe in our relationship. More importantly, it gave me hope—something I haven't had in a bit in a relationship. It made me want to look forward to seeing him every moment! That is a fantastic feeling!

The holidays came and went. On New Year's Eve day, we attend his friend's party to watch our local Ravens game. The party was fine. However, I was ignored the whole time. He really never should have attended the party. His mother had been in the hospital between Christmas and New Year very unexpectedly; his mind was elsewhere, he was very preoccupied. Someone even commented that he was grumpy, and he was. Fortunately, or unfortunately, we're both Cancers of the Zodiac sign. We are both sensitive, emotional, and moody individuals. Time will tell, I thought.

It did not end well that New Year's Eve—our very first one, not going to lie. We worked through it. I really think he's not used to being in a normal, non-dysfunctional relationship. Oftentimes, when you've been divorced, raise kids as he and I both have, you're so used to being alone and doing things by yourself or not being considerate of another one. You don't think to ask someone to accompany you or just do simple things.

On New Year's Eve, I should have been more understanding, no doubt. Later, he admitted he just never should have gone to the party. I said perhaps you shouldn't have. His mind wasn't there. He kept checking on his mother. I fully understand all this. Why did he even invite me?

CHAPTER 29

A NEW YEAR

Here we are at the start of a new year. Can I just remind everyone that relationships take work? You have chemistry, you have values and morals in common with the person you're seeing. It's always fabulous that you both have a wonderful sense of humor, which we did, I might add!! Almost every day, he made me laugh. Simple stuff truly it was, but nonetheless it worked. I kept remembering his smile and eyes when I was not around him.

We got to know each other; we would go out with other couples; we would go out a few times for lunch by ourselves. However, often we were all around other people. Looking back, I kept requesting alone time with him. Not to be intimate per se on the physical level, but to be intimate in trying to get to know him. What makes him tick? His strengths, his weaknesses, his pet peeves. What are his expectations? What does he want? Early on, we both established we wanted a relationship. Time passes into the new year. We continue to date. He says to me oneday he's not sure he knows what he wants and I was blindsided. I was like what? We discussed all this. Multiple times, I may say.

I let him figure it out. Each time we have a little tiff, or something doesn't go right, we both take time, and he comes back, and he improves tremendously. He truly does, I notice it, and I thank him. He gave the best hugs too. You can't take those for granted!!!

Lesson: All those little things add up to the big thing that makes that person—remember that.

Oftentimes, I would think, can we really get along? We did have some differences. Forget our distance apart, he was an early riser, I'm a night owl. We all can adjust. I like to boat, and he doesn't want to have anything do with that. I asked to come up, and he preferred not to. I understand why as time went on. Only at certain times does he want to come over and I get it, mostly because of his long commute to his business another hour plus from his home in the opposite direction.

Lesson One: When two people want to make it work, they will. It will happen!

I also must say and warn everyone, both male and female.

Lesson Two: Don't listen to other people.

At one point, people were giving me advice. Dear friends of mine, but one of them who was my biggest cheerleader, has been married a number of years and has never gone through divorce to know the hurt, the pain, and how that leaves you. I still cherish her and she's my biggest cheerleader. That couple who is friends with him even suggested I start dating other people and this is one of his closest friends!! I asked her why? She never gave me an answer. I was inquiring if it was him. Is he that bad? Because on this side of town where he is from and I live, everybody thinks he's a great guy!! Don't think I didn't do my homework! LOL!

Lesson: My point here is never take the other person for granted.

We all say life is short and enjoy each day. I've made it my personal mission at the beginning of this year to thank people, mostly my direct reports. Yet, thank your friends, your family members, your kids for a text or call. They don't usually.

As time went on, I think I'm probably going to text thank you more. Thank you goes a long way. Many times, as time went on after we hung up from speaking, I would always text, thanks for the call. Or the next morning, I said it. He's calling me so much more in the beginning like every day on his way home from work and on my home way home from that other job. Somehow, he stopped doing that. I'm not sure if people get comfortable too quick? I feel like that happened to us. I was meeting all these people. I was going to the parties, holding my own, but that didn't mean I didn't want his time and attention to myself. Was that selfish? I don't think so. I figured out the real reason.

Today is Valentine's Day, it falls during the week. It is probably in the top five of my worst days of the year next to New Year's Eve. Why is that? Because I'm usually alone. Of all my years, I've been alone more than I've been with a partner, unfortunately. However, many people know I won't settle. I won't settle at all. I never have and never will! I know people who swore they haven't settled, but my own family members have settled, and it has influenced me. After a number of years of counseling, I have realized it and admitted it. Society and the media, **both** put too much emphasis on Valentine's Day. I know my ex-husband used to call it a Hallmark holiday and then my son started calling it that in his young 20s, that's so not cool.

Lee did reach out the night before Valentine's Day and stated that he wanted to go to a small water town close by us for the day the weekend after Valentine's Day and I said great! We love going there. We're there for a few hours, walk around, have a few drinks with lunch before that. He belongs to a wine club, he picks up his wine, and we go home. I look very forward to that and indeed we had fun again! He was different, more attentive, into the moment.

He texts me on Valentine's morning as he usually does, and I returned the text. Then, that Saturday comes. We get together, we go have lunch the whole nine yards that we're used to doing. Hung out. I spent the night and got a dog sitter so I don't have to drive home after a few drinks. I was getting ready to go the next morning and I said we were celebrating our Valentine's weekend, right? He replied yes. I tell him I was disappointed he got me nothing for Valentine's Day. I think this day reminds him of his former wife spending, spending, spending; she got packages like four out of seven days a week. Really?! And what do I do? I gave up shopping for Lent. LOL! Any little thing I didn't need, I didn't get. I was disappointed and I told him. If I did not, it would eat at me. Some guy friends say it was soon for him to give me anything. Other people say he should have gotten me something. I know cards are very tough to get especially for Valentine's Day. When you're first starting to date, they are awful. I was disappointed. Am I materialistic? No, not at all. Do I like nice things? Absolutely. The older I get, the harder I've worked. I do like a good brand-name purse. Also, I found out they last much longer than a season or two. I'm just disappointed—I'll get over it, I told myself.

CHAPTER 30

COMMUNICATION

Communication is a necessary and interesting part of a relationship. Without it, the relationship will be stunted. You will never grow, and people will always be disappointed. It's also about expectations and intimacy. If one party wants something and the other doesn't or anticipates something differently, disappointment arises. It is an endless cycle and learn to break it.

The relationship Lee and I had experienced communication breakdowns. I expect men to listen when we speak. I am not saying he doesn't listen or any man for that matter. However, at my old age, in the mid-5os, it took me this long to figure out how men do not always listen. Texting isn't enough; that is for short, simple exchanges. Yet, it is a tool that men can see something in black and white. It takes effort and coordination to sync and maintain schedules regularly. For instance, when you live a distance apart, have careers, homes to maintain, and family to see. This is like time management 101. It can be done with a tad of time and patience.

In January, I made plans with another divorced empty nester girlfriend to go away to San Antonio, TX, mid-March. It happened to be Saint Patrick's Day weekend and her birthday weekend as well. It only worked out that way because she had a conference in the same state, even though she's from the state where I live as well. Southwest was having a great sale, we both talked about doing this, so we did it!! I told him three times when I was going away, I thought I put it in writing more than once. I went back and searched my texts; it turns out I only did it once. From there, the whole month of March, we saw each other for two days only. One thing led to another I had plans, he had plans, he has a much busier life than I do. It's way too chaotic at times; he's there for everyone. I'm finding out (I learn more and more each day) that men who run their businesses, everything is about the business. They cannot remember these little things. Sometimes, I don't realize how good my memory is. I have a girlfriend, Tamera, who says I have a memory like an elephant. Whatever that means... my point is, I remember every little detail, like what we were wearing, the weather, the time of day.

Lesson: I am going to have to try harder and be more patient. Ladies, don't always assume men can remember like you. They are too concentrated on business to remember the other stuff. Hard lesson for me.

At the time of this writing, it is in April. Our March together was horrendous. Things just snowballed with our schedule and when I was free, he wasn't. It's not good, and we must do something about it. What should we do? Where do you go from here when you know you both could have done better? I honestly don't know.

Let me backtrack... I went on this vacation, I looked so forward to it, I saved money for it. I was ready to party and let loose. I get off the plane and I have a stomach virus. It knocked me out for a while on vacation. I was weak, I hardly drank, hardly ate, my stomach was bloated. It was awful!! I don't wish this stomach virus on my former spouse! Ha! Truly I don't wish it on anyone, just saying. On the vacation, I thought I could relax, I didn't. I don't want to say I came back just as stressed, but not how I thought I would be when I returned. Obviously, it wasn't as relaxing as I had hoped and anticipated. I did not see him, but twice in the month of March. It had been three weeks until we could make time for each other to talk. That's kind of sad. My work schedule got particularly hectic, and he had plans. We finally made time to talk.

We got together and talked about many things. Ironed out a bunch of topics, or so I thought. I never forget to look in his eyes. You just know that look, and I don't mean a sensual look like to bed you. It was different. I have prepared myself to let go, to bow out of the relationship. Ladies, I braced myself, I don't want to let go, but something just is off.

Lesson: Gentlemen, don't let a good thing slip away.

Both parties must have boundaries for their own sanity. I feel taken for granted, unappreciated. Don't do that with the person you're dating. I'm not saying say I love you right away.

Lesson: Concentrate on the positive. ALWAYS!!

Lee always did that, and he taught me to do that. He was my biggest cheerleader when I was laid off. I lost my self-confidence, and no longer believed in myself, both professionally and personally. I'm still trying to continually be positive. I thought we figured things out and said we would communicate better and work out our schedules.

The following weekend is Easter. As luck has it, his family is going out at 5:00 p.m. to a local restaurant on the Saturday evening prior to Easter Sunday. I am an Irishman with no Irish luck. My mother's birthday is on the Saturday before Easter, so I take her and her boyfriend out to dinner for her birthday. Needless to say, I did not see him on that Saturday. I was hoping and thought I would see him on Easter. I heard from him Friday night twice and on Saturday, he called and texted. We talked three times in 24 hours, and I told him my plan of how I was going to make an Easter dinner on Saturday, and hand it off to my mother in the parking lot as we leave the restaurant.

What happens next? My heart is so lonely.

Lesson: Don't fail to communicate. Don't take anyone for granted. Work through it and communicate!

I will go on to say don't get frustrated or impatient. Please do not do what I did! I lost him for a bit. He forgot when I was going away and he admitted that when we talked before Easter, and he forgot. What happens next? I am in church for Easter Sunday, and I receive a Happy Easter GIF from my ex-boyfriend, Jaime. I do nothing, like it was read, nor do I respond. I really believe that put me in a bad mood. All I wanted was for my current boyfriend to ask me to be with him on Easter. During church again, I get a text from Lee that states Happy Easter! I wait until I get home to respond as I didn't want to text in church. I reply, same to you.

About an hour and a half later, he calls me. He asked me what I was doing that day. Keep in mind that it is Easter. It's like I never mentioned it; I felt like I was in the twilight zone. It did not go well, and I sat here by myself on Easter. Neither of my children came home.

.I've talked to girlfriends, they say that happens. These are the married women who have been married for a number of years. Men are like this. Then, I went back to see my counselor, who happened to be male. He admitted this is how men are!!! What didn't I know all these years? Some men are better than others no doubt. I have to be **more patient**. I have learned through this process. Just because I have a memory of an elephant doesn't mean everyone is like me.

Lesson: Let me tell you men out there if you are reading this book... communicate, communicate, communicate and I'll follow it up with listen, listen, and listen. Repeat if necessary.

We had a total breakdown in communication. I should have said I really want to see you when he called me, not get frustrated. It certainly did not help that my ex-boyfriend of over three years contacted me right before this guy called. Was I in a foul mood... probably? Yet, I still felt rejected when the current boyfriend didn't even say he wanted to see me.

Lesson: However, I will say to all the men out there... sometimes us ladies just have to keep building you up a little bit more.

Let me continue the story... I get a call the Monday after Easter, which happens to be April Fool's Day. Maybe that should have been a sign to me? I said to him I was really disappointed I didn't get to see you on Easter, and the response was sometimes these things happen.

We spoke for almost an hour. It was a fantastic conversation! The way we used to!!! It was all good and I had hope. I'm waiting for him to say, let's get together this weekend, since it would have been two weeks we're coming up on and wouldn't see each other. All he is repeating is he's got to get the oil changed in one of his cars. I was like OK, so you make an appointment for it. That doesn't mean I can't see you for lunch, a dinner, something, and he brought nothing up! I was astounded. It's like no one taught him how to date. However, he's a wonderful provider and has many, many other wonderful qualities. I attribute it to him marrying so young, at the age of 20. And yes, he has dated since. I got frustrated when we hung up, I try to go to sleep, and I couldn't. My mind is wandering and the overthinking kicks in. The next day I don't get my usual good morning text or have a great day or be careful or watch the traffic or any other little thing he would text me. I absolutely adored, absolutely adored those texts!! I thought I told him, and I know I thanked him.

I get the usual text. Nothing about getting together the upcoming weekend. I was extremely disappointed AND felt rejected. I make a mistake...I learned the hard way, ladies and gentlemen. I don't want you to follow in my footsteps.

Lesson: Never tell your partner you are not happy.

I made that mistake. I told a man that I'm not happy via text which is absolutely horrific. It depends on how you look at this. Some men would take that as—well, I better step up and figure this out or others that have been tremendously hurt shrink back in their shells even more. They think I can't make this person happy. How can I even try? Why is she bugging me? Why are we even dating? When I sent that text, I started World War III, but I didn't know it. He replied, please stop with the text, I have a business to run. I got shut down completely. I did!!! Then, I never heard from him for another three weeks. I did not call him; he did not call me. I waited a week and the following week. I was sending him good morning texts like he would say to me. He would reply, but it was done. I'm thinking, OK, he's replying. We're going to figure this out, and then I lost hope.

His responses to my text were very short, but I still I thought we had a chance.

Lesson Two: Ladies, let me tell you this is one of the worst things you can do for any relationship, tell the person you are not happy—a heterosexual relationship, a relationship with the child, a relationship with a parent and any friend in between.

I proceed to go out with a girlfriend to hear a band very last minute at a local bar on my side of town. I see him annihilated; it was awful. He wasn't handling things well. After that, I wait a few days, and finally, I got up the guts. I called him. He did not pick up, then I texted that I called and goodnight. He replied right away that he was busy on a call, and he would call me the following night.

He does call. It had been three weeks since we had spoken at all. When we finally spoke, it was the usual hi, how you are doing with two people who hadn't exchanged pleasantries.

He states... Are you ready for this one? I DON'T KNOW WHAT I WANT (Mr. IDKWIW). He says this three times in a 20-minute phone conversation. I am stunned, to say the least. We both discussed that we didn't want marriage. You know, living together or getting there takes time. I know that. We both wanted a relationship, we discussed it multiple times, he told me, his sister, and friends. He told me he didn't want to hold me back. WTH?

Can I just ask what the heck that means? I really want to know. He thought I was a nice girl and all that. Really? OK I told him we talked about all this, and he didn't say anything I said I told him I never would have introduced him to my young adult children if I didn't think this wasn't going somewhere because they're still my children and they don't need to meet people unless it's going somewhere.

Now let me remind you that I met two sets of his friends. One group from his hometown, kind of near where I live, that he's known for over 4o years, and another set around his current neighborhood. I met his two adult children; one has a girlfriend, and they live together. I met the other adult one, who's married and has two young sons. Met two out of three sisters along with his 8o-year-old mother! I said to him on the phone why did you introduce me to all these people for me to hear you don't know what you want!? Am I wrong, gentlemen, ladies? Anybody reading this? I just want to know.

I was astonished and I thought, OK, this is little blip in the road, I left him alone, and I never heard from him. I really wanted him to come to my son's graduation party that I invited him to six weeks prior. He never showed up because we were not talking to one another. A few days after the graduation party, I texted you missed a great party. It was a fun time! He responds I'm glad everything went well. That was that.

I would be lying if I said I didn't miss him. I miss him all the time. It's the little things, and if you can make it through the little things, you have got the big things covered.

I never met a gentleman as much as he was a gentleman—never ever EVER! If I never see him again or speak to him again, who knows?. Maybe when this book will actually get published, he'll read it and figure out how I felt. But something inside of me tells me hopefully he and I will reunite.

For now, I decided I will keep very busy and live my life. He made me laugh; he supported me. I met him when I was laid off and got another job. I didn't like that job and he just supported me. You know when you have a mate and someone you can lean on! Nothing else matters.

Lesson: Once again, there are few lessons to learn.1) Communicate, communicate, and communicate and I will follow up by saying listen, listen, listen. It's not the quantity of time rather than the quality of time.2) Be patient. With each other in every way. Take a minute, take a breath and regroup.3) Never ever EVER take one another for granted and certainly in doing that, never text something because you can't take it back.

CONCLUSION

So, where does one who is divorced go from here? There are too many questions and not enough answers. Let me tell you what I do know and have learned the hard way. Please let me save you time, energy, and heartache.

When you find someone who shares your values, brightens your day, and is your cheerleader, don't take that for granted. Treasure that moment despite being frustrated with them! Talk it out and communicate. Have those very blunt and direct conversations, even if you need a glass of wine to do so in a calm environment. If I knew then, what I knew now, I would be smiling every day. It's different than having a girlfriend or buddy who has your back. You just can't explain it when you had those moments together, however brief it was!

More important, I choose for each and every one of us out there who has gone through a divorce to be happy with a significant other AGAIN! As my young adult children tell me, YOLO, Mom! I had to ask what that meant... you only live once! It seems this younger generation has realized that. Yet, I hope they, like their parents' generation, find true love as well. I do believe COVID has affected each generation differently. If I thought online dating was for those of middle age, those college-aged and above are grasping their phones for those apps. Technology has improved our lives; yet, it has also set us back. We are hiding behind a screen of some sort, be it a laptop, iPad or phone. Don't be shy! Let your true self shine in a face-to-face conversation; meet up in person. Look into each other's eyes, enjoy an experience. Something as simple as a walk in a park with a picnic tells a lot about a person.

I Online dating can be fun, and it is all about how you approach it. You must be cautious of many items, especially scammers. I know enough couples that it has worked out for, and they are all extremely happy!!! Kudos for them! I am kind of jealous, I must admit. One girlfriend, Jayna, even admits, online dating is like having a second job. Each night after work, hitting the gym, and dinner, searching online was her pastime.

Keep in mind—one must re-group after a breakup though. I know too many people who jumped into a relationship very quickly after one ended. They never took a moment for introspection and healing. Some people, including myself, do not mind seeking out a counselor. My counselor tells me, "You are not as bad as you think you are!" I asked can I put that on a post it in cube? See, I crack myself up!

Other people I know are adamantly against going to counseling for themselves. While I respect that, each of us must take steps to heal, learn, and grow in that order. If you do one of these without the others, nothing is gained. Laugh at yourself.

God made each of us unique. If we were the same, life would be completely boring. Find that special someone where you have commonalities, but the differences make you respect the other more. That's where the A word comes in—appreciation. Will I ever find someone as of this writing who wants and respects Lynn for who she truly is—from her sense of humor to peacock hair in the morning? I certainly hope so! Until I do, each day I count my blessings and trust in the plan. Did I expect this to be my life as an empty nester? Heck, no! I am happy with me right now. Find joy wherever that may take you.

As a person who wanted people to learn and love again post-divorce, always have faith. Have faith in people, in relationships, and in yourself. True love is out there. I know it and feel it! I guess that is the romantic in me. My two worst days of the year are New Year's Eve and Valentine's Day. You know what? It may have taken me until mid-50s, but I got this. It's another day! On those days, give yourself an extra special treat. It doesn't mean spending money either. I'm not saying get a massage or have a spa day. Rather, have a great cup of coffee at home and read a book. Take time to meditate and enjoy the peace within yourself.

Though dating may seem draining, it is not with the right person! Be open and vulnerable to love and you never know what may happen. Take down those walls and laugh! You pass someone who caught your attention, wink at them.

Lesson: Gentlemen, always be a gentlemen and respect women. Ladies, show appreciation to your man and smile! When each of us do these simple gestures, love blossoms.

No matter what season, love is in the air. Take a moment, find joy, and be comfortable with yourself.

Lesson: Love yourself first, no matter what, and watch how that energy radiates.

Feel free to reach and send me your thoughts, positive or negative, agreeing or disagreeing. I would love to hear your story. Shall I write again to see if I ever found love?

www.ingramcontent.com/pod-product-compliance
Lightning Source LLC
Chambersburg PA
CBHW021616120626
46545CB00001B/255